THE

HANDBOOK

OF

HEARTBREAK

THE
HANDBOOK
OF
HEARTBREAK

◆

*101 Poems of Lost Love
and Sorrow*

◆

Collected by
ROBERT PINSKY

ROB WEISBACH BOOKS

William Morrow and Company, Inc.

New York

Published by Rob Weisbach Books
An Imprint of William Morrow and Company, Inc.
1350 Avenue of the Americas, New York, N.Y. 10019
www.williammorrow.com

Library of Congress Cataloging-in-Publication Data

The handbook of heartbreak : 101 poems of lost love and sorrow /
  collected by Robert Pinsky. — 1st ed.
    p.   cm.
  ISBN 0-688-16286-X (alk. paper)
  1. Loss (Psychology)—Poetry.   2. American poetry.   3. English
poetry.   I. Pinsky, Robert.
PS595.L57H36   1998
808.81'9353—dc21   98-34190
                                                                CIP

Printed in the United States of America

First Edition

1   2   3   4   5   6   7   8   9   10

BOOK DESIGN BY JO ANNE METSCH

To Biz, Caroline, Ellen,
George, Kent, Nicole
and Sam

CONTENTS

WESTERN WIND / *Anonymous (fifteenth century)*   1

LOVE SONG / *William Carlos Williams (1883–1963)*   2

NEVER AGAIN WOULD BIRDS' SONG BE THE SAME /
   Robert Frost (1874–1963)   3

ROSES ONLY / *Marianne Moore (1887–1972)*   4

PRIVILEGE OF BEING / *Robert Hass (b. 1941)*   5

WHO'S ON FIRST? / *Lloyd Schwartz (b. 1941)*   7

THEY FLEE FROM ME / *Thomas Wyatt (1503–1542)*   10

AND IF I DID WHAT THEN? /
   George Gascoigne (ca. 1535–1577)   11

ONE ART / *Elizabeth Bishop (1911–1979)*   12

ADAM'S CURSE / *William Butler Yeats (1865–1939)*   13

MEN LOVED WHOLLY BEYOND WISDOM /
   Louise Bogan (1897–1970)   15

DOING THIS / *Tony Hoagland (b. 1953)*   16

MY PICTURE LEFT IN SCOTLAND /
   Ben Jonson (1573–1637)   18

MY LIFE BY SOMEBODY ELSE / *Mark Strand (b. 1934)*   19

UNFORTUNATE COINCIDENCE /
   Dorothy Parker (1893–1967)   20

LOVE SONG: I AND THOU / *Alan Dugan (b. 1923)*   21

ASTROPHEL AND STELLA, 31 (*"With how sad steps,
   Oh Moon, thou climb'st the skies"*) / *Philip Sidney
   (1554–1586)*   22

Caelica, LXIX ("When all this All doth pass from age to age") / Fulke Greville (1554–1628)   23

SONNETS, 94 ("They that have power to hurt and will do none") / William Shakespeare (1564–1616)   24

MODERN LOVE, 17 ("At dinner, she is hostess, I am host") / George Meredith (1828–1909)   25

NEUTRAL TONES / Thomas Hardy (1840–1928)   26

THE APPARITION / John Donne (1572–1631)   27

SONG ("How sweet I roam'd from field to field") / William Blake (1757–1827)   28

SONG ("Why so pale and wan, fond lover?") / John Suckling (1609–1642)   29

EROS TURANNOS / Edwin Arlington Robinson (1869–1935)   30

SONNET XIX ("Methought I saw my late espoused saint") / John Milton (1608–1674)   32

STELLA'S BIRTH-DAY: MARCH 13, 172⁶⁄₇ / Jonathan Swift (1667–1745)   33

A SLUMBER DID MY SPIRIT SEAL / William Wordsworth (1770–1850)   36

DEATH OF THE DAY / Walter Savage Landor (1775–1864)   37

THIS LIVING HAND / John Keats (1795–1821)   38

249 ("Wild Nights—Wild Nights!") / Emily Dickinson (1830–1886)   39

305 ("The difference between Despair") / Emily Dickinson (1830–1886)   40

THE VOICE / Thomas Hardy (1840–1928)   41

SONNET ("*Thou art indeed just, Lord, if I contend*") /
    Gerard Manley Hopkins (1844–1889)   42

HELEN / *H.D.* (1886–1961)   43

THE BROTHERS / *Edwin Muir* (1887–1959)   44

BELLS FOR JOHN WHITESIDE'S DAUGHTER /
    John Crowe Ransom (1888–1974)   46

CAPTAIN CARPENTER /
    John Crowe Ransom (1888–1974)   47

SIMPLE AUTUMNAL / *Louise Bogan* (1897–1970)   50

NOT WAVING BUT DROWNING /
    Stevie Smith (1902–1971)   51

LINES WRITTEN DURING A PERIOD OF INSANITY /
    William Cowper (1731–1800)   52

THE POET'S TASK / *Pablo Neruda* (1904–1973),
    translated by Alfred Corn (b. 1943)   53

A PLAGUE OF STARLINGS /
    Robert Hayden (1913–1980)   54

THE DREAM SONGS, 14 ("*Life, friends, is boring. We
    must not say so*") / *John Berryman* (1914–1972)   56

THE DREAM SONGS, 29 ("*There sat down, once, a
    thing on Henry's heart*") /
    John Berryman (1914–1972)   57

THE INLAND LIGHTHOUSE /
    James McMichael (b. 1939)   58

KITCHENETTE BUILDING /
    Gwendolyn Brooks (b. 1917)   59

SKUNK HOUR / *Robert Lowell* (1917–1977)   60

MY MOTHER WOULD BE A FALCONRESS /
    Robert Duncan (1919–1988) — 62

GET IT AGAIN / *Mark Halliday (b. 1949)* — 65

BRILLIANCE / *Mark Doty (b. 1953)* — 68

THAT EVENING AT DINNER / *David Ferry (b. 1924)* — 71

MEASURING THE TYGER / *Jack Gilbert (b. 1925)* — 74

THE DAY LADY DIED / *Frank O'Hara (1926–1966)* — 75

LADY LAZARUS / *Sylvia Plath (1932–1963)* — 76

SPITE—HOMAGE TO SYLVIA PLATH /
    Lynn Emanuel (b. 1949) — 80

BODY / *James Merrill (1926–1995)* — 81

THE DEFINITION OF LOVE /
    Andrew Marvell (1621–1678) — 82

TEACHERS / *W. S. Merwin (b. 1927)* — 84

MEMORY UNSETTLED / *Thom Gunn (b. 1929)* — 85

FRAGMENT / *C. K. Williams (b. 1936)* — 86

IN HOUSTON / *Gail Mazur (b. 1937)* — 87

"OUT, OUT—" / *Robert Frost (1874–1963)* — 89

THE YOKE / *Frank Bidart (b. 1939)* — 91

THE WINDOW / *Lynda Hull (1954–1994)* — 92

ROUND / *Robert Pinsky (b. 1940)* — 96

MOCK ORANGE / *Louise Glück (b. 1943)* — 97

PERSONALS / *C. D. Wright (b. 1949)* — 98

HOW I GOT THIS WAY / *Patricia Traxler (b. 1944)* — 99

FRIENDS WHO HAVE FAILED /
Alan Williamson (b. 1944) 101

"BOY 'CARRYING-IN' BOTTLES IN GLASS WORKS" /
Michael Ryan (b. 1945) 102

WATCHING *SHOAH* IN A HOTEL ROOM IN AMERICA
/ *Adam Zagajewski (b. 1945), translated by Renata
Gorczynski, Benjamin Ivry, and C. K. Williams* 103

DOLOR / *Theodore Roethke (1908–1963)* 105

INSOMNIA / *Jane Kenyon (1947–1995)* 106

FACING IT / *Yusef Komunyakaa (b. 1947)* 107

OLD JOKE / *Alan Shapiro (b. 1952)* 108

LAMENTATION ON UR / *Tom Sleigh (b. 1953)* 110

OZYMANDIAS / *Percy Bysshe Shelley (1792–1822)* 111

THEY FEED THEY LION / *Philip Levine (b. 1928)* 112

MEMPHIS BLUES / *Sterling A. Brown (1901–1989)* 114

NIGHT WASH / *Anne Winters (b. 1939)* 117

MY GRANDMOTHER'S LOVE LETTERS /
Hart Crane (1899–1932) 119

THE WEARY BLUES / *Langston Hughes (1902–1967)* 120

ELEGY ON THE DEATH OF SIDNEY /
Edward Dyer (1543–1607) 122

RALEGH'S HISTORY OF THE WORLD, AN EPITAPH
FOR BENT / *Suzanne Qualls (b. 1951)* 124

SONG ON PORCELAIN / *Czesław Miłosz (b. 1911),
translated by Robert Pinsky* 125

MID-TERM BREAK / *Seamus Heaney (b. 1939)* 127

ON MY FIRST SON / *Ben Jonson (1573–1637)*   128

WAVING GOOD-BY / *Gerald Stern (b. 1925)*   129

ELEGY FOR JANE / *Theodore Roethke (1908–1963)*   130

LAST HIRED / *Mark Turpin (b. 1953)*   131

341 (*"After great pain, a formal feeling comes—"*) /
Emily Dickinson (1830–1886)   133

ENGLISH I / *David Gewanter (b. 1954)*   134

BODY, REMEMBER.... /
*Constantine Cavafy (1863–1933), translated by
Edmund Keeley and Phillip Sherrard*   136

CORTÈGE / *Carl Phillips (b. 1959)*   137

A LITANY IN TIME OF PLAGUE /
Thomas Nashe (1567–1601)   145

THE BUSINESS OF FANCYDANCING /
Sherman Alexie (b. 1966)   147

TICHBORNE'S ELEGY / *Chidiock Tichborne (d. 1586)*   149

CHURCH MONUMENTS / *George Herbert (1593–1633)*   150

MADAME LA FLEURIE / *Wallace Stevens (1879–1955)*   151

WHAT HE THOUGHT / *Heather McHugh (b. 1948)*   152

INTRODUCTION

> Western wind, when will thou blow,
>   The small rain down can rain?
> Christ, that my love were in my arms
>   And I in my bed again!

It is the lack of rain, it is the longing for a relieving western wind, it is the absence of love and the desire for one's own bed, that make this old, anonymous poem so penetrating. The lines feed my soul, but how? This is one of the great human mysteries: why do works of art about bad things such as loss and deprivation make us feel good?

Like the movie screen depicting a maniac in a hockey mask carving people up with a chain saw; like *Hamlet* with its killings and suicides and fratricide and incestuous adultery; like all the violence, family strife, and catastrophic sex in Sophocles or on TV or in the Bible—these one hundred and one poems (the number chosen because it sounds lonely to me) about the misery of loss, the sadness risked by every love or attachment, can please the reader mightily. They are beautiful, and they offer a deep satisfaction—and yet they are about feeling the opposite of satisfaction.

Perhaps even more than drama or film, works that rely mainly on words produced by a voice, as in poetry or song, frequently seem to rely for their material on the unhappy parts of life, in order to give us the joy of art. The great songs and poems about joy in life do exist, but they are outnumbered by those in which somebody does somebody wrong. Oh what a beautiful morning has been said in song, but more often we prefer to look wistfully over the rainbow, or happily consider the tale of Frankie and Johnny, the complaint that smoke gets in your eyes, or that I can't get no satisfaction.

The great answers to this mystery probably have, each of them, a measure of truth: by the artist's gift, we have our own unarticulated feeling expressed; by catharsis we get the woe and the fear of woe out of our system; by sublimation we convert neediness into a possession; by recognition we feel companionship; by contrast we relish recollected or imagined misery because it heightens the tranquillity of our present state; and because we are not, at the moment, being attacked by chain saw or betrayed by our beloved, we can take voyeuristic, secure pleasure in the spectacle.

To express an emotion feels so good that I think there is a kind of evolutionary imperative behind that feeling. The human animal, according to a classical notion, has claws and teeth that are pathetic as weapons, a hide that provides scant protection, with its thin fur; the creature cannot run very fast or swim very well, and it cannot fly at all, nor is it strong. It has survived by cooperating: using an astonishingly complex system of grunts as a language to communicate not only with its peers but with its ancestors and descendants.

By means of the rhymes and rhythms of poetry, by means of song and dance, the creature can communicate even with those who are absent: far away, or dead, or not yet born. The African *griots* in Alex Haley's *Roots* can recount dynasties, property rights, genealogies reaching back centuries, because they have mastered the elaborate techniques of their poetic art. They are experts in a technology that takes for its medium the breath inside the human body itself.

Maybe some of the pleasure we take in a somebody-done-somebody-wrong song has to do with that technology, with its ancient roots in our evolution. Like ants and bees we are a social animal, but we are a cultural animal as well. That is, we do not merely gather in the hive of our family, town, city—we learn the changing customs and musics and slangs of the place as well, making those cultural materials and unmaking them from generation to generation, from minute to minute. We make things up, and we express ourselves, as part of who we are, and in particular as part of how we are together, with one another.

The song of loneliness for my love and my bed, the lament I chant for the wind and rain, reminds me of my connection to all the other people who know my language, who know language itself, who can recognize in the cadences of my lament a work of art, though we may not call it that. To say the words of a poem is a physical and emotional comfort, as well as a genetically reinforced thrill; it is a little like being actually, physically touched or embraced. If the words say what I lack or miss or long for, then the comfort and the thrill are perhaps that much more penetrating because they remind me of how the physical act of speech can connect me to other people.

All art is imitation, says Aristotle: poetry imitates speaking and being spoken to in response. Love poetry, for example, imitates speech with the beloved, and sometimes the imitation is more powerful for us than the actuality. Other times, the imitation seems to help us approach the awesome power of the actuality.

Love is a tyrant, as Edwin Arlington Robinson implies by the title of his poem "Eros Turannos." But as Robinson acknowledges, Love is also a god, and to contend with a god confers a certain elevation. So if poetry imitates speech, love poetry imitates speech with a god who inspires awe. "Eros Turannos" in its early stanzas tells about a woman who chooses a disastrous love rather than no love at all. The closing stanzas place that woman in the context of a community. The poem begins:

> She fears him, and will always ask
>   What fated her to choose him;
> She meets in his engaging mask
>   All reasons to refuse him;
> But what she meets and what she fears
> Are less than are the downward years,
> Drawn slowly to the foamless weirs
>   Of age, were she to lose him.
>
> Between a blurred sagacity
>   That once had power to sound him,
> And Love, that will not let him be
>   The Judas that she found him,
> Her pride assuages her almost,
> As if it were alone the cost.—

He sees that he will not be lost,
>   And waits and looks around him.

This unworthy man has her where he wants her, and things come out badly, as part of her knew they would. The final stanzas introduce the rather unexpected element of her neighbors, a community, a whole town that has vibrated to her seclusion:

>   We tell you, tapping on our brows,
>   The story as it should be,—
>   As if the story of a house
>   Were told, or ever could be;
>   We'll have no kindly veil between
>   Her visions and those we have seen,—
>   As if we guessed what hers have been,
>   Or what they are or would be.
>
>   Meanwhile we do no harm; for they
>   That with a god have striven,
>   Not hearing much of what we say,
>   Take what the god has given;
>   Though like waves breaking it may be,
>   Or like a changed familiar tree,
>   Or like a stairway to the sea
>   Where down the blind are driven.

In some way, Robinson's amazing rhymes are like the town's attention, in that they give this story an awful dignity. The woman's story means more because the town and the poem have recounted that story. And the town has gained something, too, because this wrestling with a god has taken place within its ken. The individual suffering and the communal taking note of that suffering: the poem widens out from the sad love story of its beginning.

A widening process something like that structure of "Eros Turannos," moving from individual pain outward to communal concerns, has guided my organization of this book. I begin more or less at the narrow end of a funnel (the image of a twister storm comes to mind), with poems strictly about romantic love-misery, and gradually, unsystematically widen the scope to include a broader range of loss and comfort, sorrow and its expression. In the Wallace Stevens poem that supplies this book's title, the love is for earth itself: that "bearded queen," our mother; and the earth itself is also the handbook where we seek illumination.

I hope that reading from that great handbook alongside the poets gathered here in this book will be, for the reader, a thrill and a solace.

>   —Robert Pinsky
>   Truro, Massachusetts
>   July 20, 1998

WESTERN WIND

Western wind, when will thou blow,
  The small rain down can rain?
Christ, that my love were in my arms
  And I in my bed again!

—ANONYMOUS

LOVE SONG

I lie here thinking of you:—

the stain of love
is upon the world!
Yellow, yellow, yellow
it eats into the leaves,
smears with saffron
the horned branches that lean
heavily
against a smooth purple sky!
There is no light
only a honey-thick stain
that drips from leaf to leaf
and limb to limb
spoiling the colors
of the whole world—
you far off there under
the wine-red selvage of the west!

—WILLIAM CARLOS WILLIAMS

NEVER AGAIN WOULD BIRDS' SONG BE THE SAME

He would declare and could himself believe
That the birds there in all the garden round
From having heard the daylong voice of Eve
Had added to their own an oversound,
Her tone of meaning but without the words.
Admittedly an eloquence so soft
Could only have had an influence on birds
When call or laughter carried it aloft.
Be that as may be, she was in their song.
Moreover her voice upon their voices crossed
Had now persisted in the woods so long
That probably it never would be lost.
Never again would birds' song be the same.
And to do that to birds was why she came.

—ROBERT FROST

ROSES ONLY

You do not seem to realise that beauty is a liability rather than
an asset—that in view of the fact that spirit creates form we are justified in supposing
that you must have brains. For you, a symbol of the unit, stiff and sharp,
conscious of surpassing by dint of native superiority and liking for everything
self-dependent, anything an

ambitious civilisation might produce: for you, unaided to attempt through sheer
reserve, to confute presumptions resulting from observation, is idle. You
cannot make us
think you a delightful happen-so. But rose, if you are brilliant, it
is not because your petals are the without-which-nothing of pre-eminence. You would, minus thorns,
look like a what-is-this, a mere

peculiarity. They are not proof against a worm, the elements, or mildew
but what about the predatory hand? What is brilliance without co-ordination? Guarding the
infinitesimal pieces of your mind, compelling audience to
the remark that it is better to be forgotten than to be remembered too violently,
your thorns are the best part of you.

—MARIANNE MOORE

PRIVILEGE OF BEING

Many are making love. Up above, the angels
in the unshaken ether and crystal of human longing
are braiding one another's hair, which is strawberry blond
and the texture of cold rivers. They glance
down from time to time at the awkward ecstasy—
it must look to them like featherless birds
splashing in the spring puddle of a bed—
and then one woman, she is about to come,
peels back the man's shut eyelids and says,
look at me, and he does. Or is it the man
tugging the curtain rope in that dark theater?
Anyway, they do, they look at each other;
two beings with evolved eyes, rapacious,
startled, connected at the belly in an unbelievably sweet
lubricious glue, stare at each other,
and the angels are desolate. They hate it. They shudder pathetically
like lithographs of Victorian beggars
with perfect features and alabaster skin hawking rags
in the lewd alleys of the novel.
All of creation is offended by this distress.
It is like the keening sound the moon makes sometimes,
rising. The lovers especially cannot bear it,
it fills them with unspeakable sadness, so that
they close their eyes again and hold each other, each
feeling the mortal singularity of the body
they have enchanted out of death for an hour or so,
and one day, running at sunset, the woman says to the man,
I woke up feeling so sad this morning because I realized
that you could not, as much as I love you,
dear heart, cure my loneliness,
wherewith she touched his cheek to reassure him
that she did not mean to hurt him with this truth.

And the man is not hurt exactly,
he understands that life has limits, that people
die young, fail at love,
fail of their ambitions. He runs beside her, he thinks
of the sadness they have gasped and crooned their way out of
coming, clutching each other with old, invented
forms of grace and clumsy gratitude, ready
to be alone again, or dissatisfied, or merely
companionable like the couples on the summer beach
reading magazine articles about intimacy between the sexes
to themselves, and to each other,
and to the immense, illiterate, consoling angels.

—ROBERT HASS

WHO'S ON FIRST?

"You can be so inconsiderate."

                              "You are too sensitive."

"Then why don't you take my feelings into consideration?"

                                                    "If you
weren't so sensitive it wouldn't matter."

                    •

"You seem to really care about me only when you want me to do
something for you."

              "You do too much for people."

                    •

"I thought you were going home because you were too tired to go with
me to a bar."

              "I was. But Norman didn't want to come here alone."

                    •

"I'm awfully tired. Do you mind taking the subway home?"

                                              (*Silence.*)

"You could stay over . . ."

                    (*Silence.*)

"I'll take you home."

              (*Silence.*)

                    •

"Why do we have sex only when you want to?"

                                        "Because you want to
have sex all the time."

                    •

"Relationships work when two people equally desire to give to each
other."

        "Relationships rarely work."

                    •

"Do you love me?"

              "Of course—; but I resent it."

                    •

"Why aren't you more affectionate?"

                    "I am."

        •

"Couldn't we ever speak to each other without irony?"

                                        "Sure."

        •

"I love you, you know."

                    "Yes . . . but why?"

        •

"Do you resent my advice?"

                    "Yes. Especially because you're usually right."

        •

"Why do you like these paintings?"

                              "What isn't there is more important
than what is."

        •

"Your taste sometimes seems strange to me."

                                        "I'm a Philistine."

"A real Philistine would never admit it."

                                   "I suppose you're right."

        •

"Aren't you interested in what I care about?"

                                   "Yes. But not now."

        •

"We should be more open with each other."

                                   "Yes."

"Shall we talk things over?"

                         "What is there to say?"

        •

"Are you ever going to cut down on your smoking?"

                                        "It's all right—
I don't inhale."

        •

"Sometimes I get very annoyed with you."

                                   "The world is annoying."

·

"Your cynicism is too easy."

"Words interfere with the expression
of complex realities."

·

"Do you enjoy suffering?"

"You can't work if you don't suffer."

"But we suffer anyway."

"I know."

·

"Do you think we ever learn anything?"

"I've learned to do without."

·

"You're always so negative."

"I feel death all the time."

"Are you afraid of anything?"

"Not working."

·

"What shall we do for dinner?"

"It doesn't matter—whatever you'd like."

·

"Why don't you care more?"

"I do."

—LLOYD SCHWARTZ

9

THEY FLEE FROM ME

They flee from me, that sometime did me seek,
With naked foot stalking in my chamber.
I have seen them, gentle, tame, and meek,
That now are wild, and do not remember
That sometime they put themselves in danger
To take bread at my hand; and now they range,
Busily seeking with a continual change.

Thanked be Fortune it hath been otherwise,
Twenty times better; but once in special,
In thin array, after a pleasant guise,
When her loose gown from her shoulders did fall,
And she me caught in her arms long and small,
And therewith all sweetly did me kiss
And softly said, "Dear heart, how like you this?"

It was no dream, I lay broad waking.
But all is turned, thorough my gentleness,
Into a strange fashion of forsaking;
And I have leave to go, of her goodness,
And she also to use newfangleness.
But since that I so kindly am served,
I fain would know what she hath deserved.

—THOMAS WYATT

AND IF I DID WHAT THEN?

"And if I did what then?
Are you aggrieved therefore?
The sea hath fish for every man,
And what would you have more?"

Thus did my mistress once
Amaze my mind with doubt,
And popped a question for the nonce
To beat my brains about.

Whereto I thus replied:
"Each fisherman can wish
That all the sea at every tide
Were his alone to fish.

And so did I, in vain;
But since it may not be,
Let such fish there as find the gain,
And leave the loss for me.

And with such luck and loss
I will content myself,
Till tides of turning time may toss
Such fishers on the shelf.

And when they stick on sands,
That every man may see,
Then will I laugh and clap my hands,
As they do now at me."

—GEORGE GASCOIGNE

ONE ART

The art of losing isn't hard to master;
so many things seem filled with the intent
to be lost that their loss is no disaster.

Lose something every day. Accept the fluster
of lost door keys, the hour badly spent.
The art of losing isn't hard to master.

Then practice losing farther, losing faster:
places, and names, and where it was you meant
to travel. None of these will bring disaster.

I lost my mother's watch. And look! my last, or
next-to-last, of three loved houses went.
The art of losing isn't hard to master.

I lost two cities, lovely ones. And, vaster,
some realms I owned, two rivers, a continent.
I miss them, but it wasn't a disaster.

—Even losing you (the joking voice, a gesture
I love) I shan't have lied. It's evident
the art of losing's not too hard to master
though it may look like (*Write* it!) like disaster.

—ELIZABETH BISHOP

ADAM'S CURSE

We sat together at one summer's end,
That beautiful mild woman, your close friend,
And you and I, and talked of poetry.
I said, "A line will take us hours maybe;
Yet if it does not seem a moment's thought,
Our stitching and unstitching has been naught.
Better go down upon your marrow-bones
And scrub a kitchen pavement, or break stones
Like an old pauper, in all kinds of weather;
For to articulate sweet sounds together
Is to work harder than all these, and yet
Be thought an idler by the noisy set
Of bankers, schoolmasters, and clergymen
The martyrs call the world."

                       And thereupon
That beautiful mild woman for whose sake
There's many a one shall find out all heartache
On finding that her voice is sweet and low
Replied, "To be born woman is to know—
Although they do not talk of it at school—
That we must labour to be beautiful."

I said, "It's certain there is no fine thing
Since Adam's fall but needs much labouring.
There have been lovers who thought love should be
So much compounded of high courtesy
That they would sigh and quote with learned looks
Precedents out of beautiful old books;
Yet now it seems an idle trade enough."

We sat grown quiet at the name of love;
We saw the last embers of daylight die,
And in the trembling blue-green of the sky
A moon, worn as if it had been a shell
Washed by time's waters as they rose and fell
About the stars and broke in days and years.

I had a thought for no one's but your ears:
That you were beautiful, and that I strove
To love you in the old high way of love;
That it had all seemed happy, and yet we'd grown
As weary-hearted as that hollow moon.

—WILLIAM BUTLER YEATS

MEN LOVED WHOLLY BEYOND WISDOM

Men loved wholly beyond wisdom
Have the staff without the banner.
Like a fire in a dry thicket
Rising within women's eyes
Is the love men must return.
Heart, so subtle now, and trembling,
What a marvel to be wise,
To love never in this manner!
To be quiet in the fern
Like a thing gone dead and still,
Listening to the prisoned cricket
Shake its terrible, dissembling
Music in the granite hill.

—LOUISE BOGAN

DOING THIS

I'm driving back and forth
on the gravel lane
before the two-room, stucco house

of the woman I love. She's inside,
making love with a woman
whose white car is parked in the driveway

and it, this car, disturbs me
more than anything. It sticks out of itself
so far into my life. Each time I pass,

I know, with a ten-pound sadness in my chest,
that I can't keep doing this.
And now I realize, far too late,

I should have fought for her, should have
wept and begged and made the full,
hair-extracting spectacle

of what I felt. I should have
shed my pride.
What good is pride? When you die,

I know they turn you
inside out, to see what portion
of your god-allotted guts

you failed to spend on earth.
The ones who arrive in heaven
without a kopek of their fortune left

are welcomed, cheered, embraced.
The rest are chastised and reborn
as salesmen and librarians.

It's so simple,
and that's what gets me—that every time
I drive up and down this street,

looking at that white Toyota in the drive,
it messes up not just this life,
but my eternity as well.

But I keep doing it,
dragging myself back and forth
over this corner of the world

which scrapes and grinds against me,
like a rock on the bow of a ship.
Etching the errors in my surface

deeper, and deeper. And less forgiven.

—TONY HOAGLAND

MY PICTURE LEFT IN SCOTLAND

I now think Love is rather deaf than blind,
    For else it could not be
        That she
Whom I adore so much should so slight me,
    And cast my love behind;
I'm sure my language to her was as sweet,
        And every close did meet
      In sentence of as subtle feet,
        As hath the youngest he
    That sits in shadow of Apollo's tree.

    Oh, but my conscious fears
        That fly my thoughts between,
        Tell me that she hath seen
        My hundred of grey hairs,
        Told seven-and-forty years,
    Read so much waste, as she cannot embrace
    My mountain belly, and my rocky face;
And all these through her eyes have stopped her ears.

—BEN JONSON

MY LIFE BY SOMEBODY ELSE

I have done what I could but you avoid me.
I left a bowl of milk on the desk to tempt you.
Nothing happened. I left my wallet there, full of money.
You must have hated me for that. You never came.

I sat at my typewriter naked, hoping you would wrestle me
to the floor. I played with myself just to arouse you.
Boredom drove me to sleep. I offered you my wife.
I sat her on the desk and spread her legs. I waited.

The days drag on. The exhausted light falls like a bandage
over my eyes. Is it because I am ugly? Was anyone
ever so sad? It is pointless to slash my wrists. My hands
would fall off. And then what hope would I have?

Why do you never come? Must I have you by being
somebody else? Must I write *My Life* by somebody else?
My Death by somebody else? Are you listening?
Somebody else has arrived. Somebody else is writing.

—MARK STRAND

UNFORTUNATE COINCIDENCE

By the time you swear you're his,
    Shivering and sighing,
And he vows his passion is
    Infinite, undying—
Lady, make a note of this:
    One of you is lying.

            —DOROTHY PARKER

LOVE SONG: I AND THOU

Nothing is plumb, level, or square:
　　the studs are bowed, the joists
are shaky by nature, no piece fits
　　any other piece without a gap
or pinch, and bent nails
　　dance all over the surfacing
like maggots. By Christ
　　I am no carpenter. I built
the roof for myself, the walls
　　for myself, the floors
for myself, and got
　　hung up in it myself. I
danced with a purple thumb
　　at this house-warming, drunk
with my prime whiskey: rage.
　　Oh I spat rage's nails
into the frame-up of my work:
　　it held. It settled plumb,
level, solid, square and true
　　for that great moment. Then
it screamed and went on through,
　　skewing as wrong the other way.
God damned it. This is hell,
　　but I planned it, I sawed it,
I nailed it, and I
　　will live in it until it kills me.
I can nail my left palm
　　to the left-hand crosspiece but
I can't do everything myself.
　　I need a hand to nail the right,
a help, a love, a you, a wife.

—ALAN DUGAN

With how sad steps, Oh Moon, thou climb'st the skies,
How silently, and with how wan a face!
What, may it be that even in heav'nly place
That busy archer his sharp arrows tries?
Sure, if that long-with-love-acquainted eyes
Can judge of love, thou feel'st a lover's case;
I read it in thy looks: thy languished grace,
To me that feel the like, thy state descries.
Then even of fellowship, Oh Moon, tell me,
Is constant love deemed there but want of wit?
Are beauties there as proud as here they be?
Do they above love to be loved, and yet
Those lovers scorn whom that love doth possess?
Do they call virtue there ungratefulness?

—PHILIP SIDNEY

Caelica, LXIX

When all this All doth pass from age to age,
And revolution in a circle turn,
Then heavenly justice doth appear like rage,
The caves do roar, the very seas do burn,
    Glory grows dark, the sun becomes a night,
    And makes this great world feel a greater might.

When love doth change his seat from heart to heart,
And worth about the wheel of fortune goes,
Grace is diseas'd, desert seems overthwart,
Vows are forlorn, and truth doth credit lose,
    Chance then gives law, desire must be wise,
    And look more ways than one, or lose her eyes.

My age of joy is past, of woe begun,
Absence my presence is, strangeness my grace,
With them that walk against me, is my sun:
The wheel is turn'd, I hold the lowest place,
    What can be good to me since my love is,
    To do me harm, content to do amiss?

—FULKE GREVILLE

They that have power to hurt and will do none,
That do not do the thing they most do show,
Who, moving others, are themselves as stone,
Unmoved, cold, and to temptation slow;
They rightly do inherit heaven's graces
And husband nature's riches from expense;
They are the lords and owners of their faces,
Others but stewards of their excellence.
The summer's flower is to the summer sweet,
Though to itself it only live and die,
But if that flower with base infection meet,
The basest weed outbraves his dignity:

    For sweetest things turn sourest by their deeds;
    Lilies that fester smell far worse than weeds.

—WILLIAM SHAKESPEARE

MODERN LOVE, 17

At dinner, she is hostess, I am host.
Went the feast ever cheerfuller? She keeps
The Topic over intellectual deeps
In buoyancy afloat. They see no ghost.
With sparkling surface-eyes we ply the ball:
It is in truth a most contagious game:
HIDING THE SKELETON, shall be its name.
Such play as this, the devils might appal!
But here's the greater wonder; in that we
Enamoured of an acting nought can tire,
Each other, like true hypocrites, admire;
Warm-lighted looks, Love's ephemerioe,
Shoot gaily o'er the dishes and the wine.
We waken envy of our happy lot.
Fast, sweet, and golden, shows the marriage-knot.
Dear guests, you now have seen Love's corpse-light shine.

—GEORGE MEREDITH

NEUTRAL TONES

We stood by a pond that winter day,
And the sun was white, as though chidden of God,
And a few leaves lay on the starving sod;
  —They had fallen from an ash, and were gray.

Your eyes on me were as eyes that rove
Over tedious riddles of years ago;
And some words played between us to and fro
  On which lost the more by our love.

The smile on your mouth was the deadest thing
Alive enough to have strength to die;
And a grin of bitterness swept thereby
  Like an ominous bird a-wing. . . .

Since then, keen lessons that love deceives,
And wrings with wrong, have shaped to me
Your face, and the God-curst sun, and a tree,
  And a pond edged with grayish leaves.

       —THOMAS HARDY

THE APPARITION

When by thy scorn, O murderess, I am dead,
    And that thou thinkst thee free
From all solicitation from me,
Then shall my ghost come to thy bed,
And thee, fain'd vestal, in worse arms shall see;
Then thy sick taper will begin to wink,
And he, whose thou art then, being tired before,
Will, if thou stir, or pinch to wake him, think
    Thou call'st for more,
And in false sleep will from thee shrink,
And then poor Aspen wretch, neglected thou
Bath'd in a cold quicksilver sweat wilt lie
    A veryer ghost than I;
What I will say, I will not tell thee now,
Lest that preserve thee; and since my love is spent,
I'had rather thou shouldst painfully repent,
Then by my threatnings rest still innocent.

—JOHN DONNE

SONG

How sweet I roam'd from field to field,
  And tasted all the summer's pride,
'Till I the prince of love beheld,
  Who in the sunny beams did glide!

He shew'd me lilies for my hair,
  And blushing roses for my brow;
He led me through his gardens fair,
  Where all his golden pleasures grow.

With sweet May dews my wings were wet,
  And Phœbus fir'd my vocal rage;
He caught me in his silken net,
  And shut me in his golden cage.

He loves to sit and hear me sing,
  Then, laughing, sports and plays with me;
Then stretches out my golden wing,
  And mocks my loss of liberty.

—WILLIAM BLAKE

SONG

Why so pale and wan, fond lover?
   Prithee, why so pale?
Will, when looking well can't move her,
   Looking ill prevail?
   Prithee, why so pale?

Why so dull and mute, young sinner?
   Prithee, why so mute?
Will, when speaking well can't win her,
   Saying nothing do 't?
   Prithee, why so mute?

Quit, quit, for shame; this will not move,
   This cannot take her.
If of herself she will not love,
   Nothing can make her:
   The devil take her!

—JOHN SUCKLING

EROS TURANNOS

She fears him, and will always ask
    What fated her to choose him;
She meets in his engaging mask
    All reasons to refuse him;
But what she meets and what she fears
Are less than are the downward years,
Drawn slowly to the foamless weirs
    Of age, were she to lose him.

Between a blurred sagacity
    That once had power to sound him,
And Love, that will not let him be
    The Judas that she found him,
Her pride assuages her almost,
As if it were alone the cost.—
He sees that he will not be lost,
    And waits and looks around him.

A sense of ocean and old trees
    Envelops and allures him;
Tradition, touching all he sees,
    Beguiles and reassures him;
And all her doubts of what he says
Are dimmed with what she knows of days—
Till even prejudice delays
    And fades, and she secures him.

The falling leaf inaugurates
    The reign of her confusion:
The pounding wave reverberates
    The dirge of her illusion;
And home, where passion lived and died,

Becomes a place where she can hide,
While all the town and harbor side
  Vibrate with her seclusion.

We tell you, tapping on our brows,
  The story as it should be,—
As if the story of a house
  Were told, or ever could be;
We'll have no kindly veil between
Her visions and those we have seen,—
As if we guessed what hers have been,
  Or what they are or would be.

Meanwhile we do no harm; for they
  That with a god have striven,
Not hearing much of what we say,
  Take what the god has given;
Though like waves breaking it may be,
Or like a changed familiar tree,
Or like a stairway to the sea
  Where down the blind are driven.

                    —EDWIN ARLINGTON ROBINSON

SONNET XIX

Methought I saw my late espoused saint
    Brought to me like Alcestis from the grave,
    Whom Jove's great son to her glad husband gave,
    Rescued from death by force though pale and faint.
Mine as whom washed from spot of childbed taint,
    Purification in the old Law did save,
    And such, as yet once more I trust to have
    Full sight of her in heaven without restraint,
Came vested all in white, pure as her mind:
    Her face was veiled, yet to my fancied sight,
    Love, sweetness, goodness in her person shined
So clear, as in no face with more delight.
    But O as to embrace me she inclined
    I waked, she fled, and day brought back my night.

—JOHN MILTON

STELLA'S BIRTH-DAY
March 13, 172⁶/₇

This Day, whate'er the Fates decree,
Shall still be kept with Joy by me:
This Day then, let us not be told,
That you are sick, and I grown old,
Nor think on our approaching Ills,
And talk of Spectacles and Pills;
To morrow will be Time enough
To hear such mortifying Stuff.
Yet, since from Reason may be brought
A better and more pleasing Thought,
Which can in spite of all Decays,
Support a few remaining Days:
From not the gravest of Divines,
Accept for once some serious Lines.

   Although we now can form no more
Long Schemes of Life, as heretofore;
Yet you, while Time is running fast,
Can look with Joy on what is past.

   Were future Happiness and Pain,
A mere Contrivance of the Brain,
As Atheists argue, to entice,
And fit their Proselytes for Vice;
(The only Comfort they propose,
To have Companions in their Woes.)
Grant this the Case, yet sure 'tis hard,
That Virtue, stil'd its own Reward,
And by all Sages understood
To be the chief of human Good,
Should acting, die, nor leave behind
Some lasting Pleasure in the Mind,

Which by Remembrance will assuage,
Grief, Sickness, Poverty, and Age;
And strongly shoot a radiant Dart,
To shine through Life's declining Part.

Say, *Stella*, feel you no Content,
Reflecting on a Life well spent?
Your skilful Hand employ'd to save
Despairing Wretches from the Grave;
And then supporting with your Store,
Those whom you dragg'd from Death before:
(So Providence on Mortals waits,
Preserving what it first creates)
Your gen'rous Boldness to defend
An innocent and absent Friend;
That Courage which can make you just,
To Merit humbled in the Dust:
The Detestation you express
For Vice in all its glitt'ring Dress:
That Patience under tort'ring Pain,
Where stubborn Stoicks would complain.

Shall these like empty Shadows pass,
Or Forms reflected from a Glass?
Or mere Chimæra's in the Mind,
That fly and leave no Marks behind?
Does not the Body thrive and grow
By Food of twenty Years ago?
And, had it not been still supply'd,
It must a thousand Times have dy'd.
Then, who with Reason can maintain,
That no Effects of Food remain?
And, is not Virtue in Mankind
The Nutriment that feeds the Mind?
Upheld by each good Action past,

And still continued by the last:
Then, who with Reason can pretend,
That all Effects of Virtue end?

Believe me *Stella*, when you show
That true Contempt for Things below,
Nor prize your Life for other Ends
Than merely to oblige your Friends;
Your former Actions claim their Part,
And join to fortify your Heart.
For Virtue in her daily Race,
Like *Janus*, bears a double Face;
Looks back with Joy where she has gone,
And therefore goes with Courage on.
She at your sickly Couch will wait,
And guide you to a better State.

O then, whatever Heav'n intends,
Take Pity on your pitying Friends;
Nor let your Ills affect your Mind,
To fancy they can be unkind.
Me, surely me, you ought to spare,
Who gladly would your Suff'rings share;
Or give my Scrap of Life to you,
And think it far beneath your Due;
You, to whose Care so oft I owe,
That I'm alive to tell you so.

—JONATHAN SWIFT

A SLUMBER DID MY SPIRIT SEAL

A slumber did my spirit seal;
   I had no human fears:
She seemed a thing that could not feel
   The touch of earthly years.

No motion has she now, no force;
   She neither hears nor sees;
Rolled round in earth's diurnal course,
   With rocks, and stones, and trees.

—WILLIAM WORDSWORTH

DEATH OF THE DAY

My pictures blacken in their frames
   As night comes on,
And youthful maids and wrinkled dames
   Are now all one.

Death of the day! a sterner Death
   Did worse before;
The fairest form, the sweetest breath,
   Away he bore.

—WALTER SAVAGE LANDOR

THIS LIVING HAND

This living hand, now warm and capable
Of earnest grasping, would, if it were cold
And in the icy silence of the tomb,
So haunt thy days and chill thy dreaming nights
That thou would wish thine own heart dry of blood,
So in my veins red life might stream again,
And thou be conscience-calm'd. See, here it is—
I hold it towards you.

—JOHN KEATS

249

Wild Nights—Wild Nights!
Were I with thee
Wild Nights should be
Our luxury!

Futile—the Winds—
To a Heart in port—
Done with the Compass—
Done with the Chart!

Rowing in Eden—
Ah, the Sea!
Might I but moor—Tonight—
In Thee!

—EMILY DICKINSON

The difference between Despair
And Fear—is like the One
Between the instant of a Wreck—
And when the Wreck has been—

The Mind is smooth—no Motion—
Contented as the Eye
Upon the Forehead of a Bust—
That knows—it cannot see—

—EMILY DICKINSON

THE VOICE

Woman much missed, how you call to me, call to me,
Saying that now you are not as you were
When you had changed from the one who was all to me,
But as at first, when our day was fair.

Can it be you that I hear?   Let me view you, then,
Standing as when I drew near to the town
Where you would wait for me : yes, as I knew you then,
Even to the original air-blue gown!

Or is it only the breeze, in its listlessness
Travelling across the wet mead to me here,
You being ever dissolved to wan wistlessness,
Heard no more again far or near?

   Thus I ; faltering forward,
   Leaves around me falling,
Wind oozing thin through the thorn from norward,
   And the woman calling.

—THOMAS HARDY

SONNET

Justus quidem tu es, Domine, si disputem tecum; verumtamen justa loquar ad te: Quare via impiorum prosperatur? &c.

Thou art indeed just, Lord, if I contend
With thee; but, sir, so what I plead is just.
Why do sinners' ways prosper? and why must
Disappointment all I endeavour end?

Wert thou my enemy, O thou my friend,
How wouldst thou worse, I wonder, than thou dost
Defeat, thwart me? Oh, the sots and thralls of lust
Do in spare hours more thrive than I that spend,

Sir, life upon thy cause. See, banks and brakes
Now, leavèd how thick! lacèd they are again
With fretty chervil, look, and fresh wind shakes

Them; birds build—but not I build; no, but strain,
Time's eunuch, and not breed one work that wakes.
Mine, O thou lord of life, send my roots rain.

—GERARD MANLEY HOPKINS

HELEN

All Greece hates
the still eyes in the white face,
the luster as of olives
where she stands,
And the white hands.

All Greece reviles
the wan face when she smiles,
hating it deeper still
when it grows wan and white,
remembering past enchantments
and past ills.

Greece sees unmoved,
God's daughter, born of love,
the beauty of cool feet
and slenderest knees,
could love indeed the maid,
only if she were laid,
white ash amid funereal cypresses.

—H. D.

THE BROTHERS

Last night I watched my brothers play,
The gentle and the reckless one,
In a field two yards away.
For half a century they were gone
Beyond the other side of care
To be among the peaceful dead.
Even in a dream how could I dare
Interrogate that happiness
So wildly spent yet never less?
For still they raced about the green
And were like two revolving suns;
A brightness poured from head to head,
So strong I could not see their eyes
Or look into their paradise.
What were they doing, the happy ones?
Yet where I was they once had been.

I thought, How could I be so dull,
Twenty thousand days ago,
Not to see they were beautiful?
I asked them, Were you really so
As you are now, that other day?
And the dream was soon away.

For then we played for victory
And not to make each other glad.
A darkness covered every head,
Frowns twisted the original face,
And through that mask we could not see
The beauty and the buried grace.

I have observed in foolish awe
The dateless mid-days of the law
And seen indifferent justice done
By everyone on everyone.
And in a vision I have seen
My brothers playing on the green.

—EDWIN MUIR

BELLS FOR JOHN WHITESIDE'S DAUGHTER

There was such speed in her little body,
And such lightness in her footfall,
It is no wonder her brown study
Astonishes us all.

Her wars were bruited in our high window.
We looked among orchard trees and beyond
Where she took arms against her shadow,
Or harried unto the pond

The lazy geese, like a snow cloud
Dripping their snow on the green grass,
Tricking and stopping, sleepy and proud,
Who cried in goose, Alas,

For the tireless heart within the little
Lady with rod that made them rise
From their noon apple-dreams and scuttle
Goose-fashion under the skies!

But now go the bells, and we are ready,
In one house we are sternly stopped
To say we are vexed at her brown study,
Lying so primly propped.

—JOHN CROWE RANSOM

CAPTAIN CARPENTER

Captain Carpenter rose up in his prime
Put on his pistols and went riding out
But had got wellnigh nowhere at that time
Till he fell in with ladies in a rout.

It was a pretty lady and all her train
That played with him so sweetly but before
An hour she'd taken a sword with all her main
And twined him of his nose for evermore.

Captain Carpenter mounted up one day
And rode straightway into a stranger rogue
That looked unchristian but be that as may
The Captain did not wait upon prologue.

But drew upon him out of his great heart
The other swung against him with a club
And cracked his two legs at the shinny part
And let him roll and stick like any tub.

Captain Carpenter rode many a time
From male and female took he sundry harms
He met the wife of Satan crying "I'm
The she-wolf bids you shall bear no more arms."

Their strokes and counters whistled in the wind
I wish he had delivered half his blows
But where she should have made off like a hind
The bitch bit off his arms at the elbows.

And Captain Carpenter parted with his ears
To a black devil that used him in this wise
O Jesus ere his threescore and ten years
Another had plucked out his sweet blue eyes.

Captain Carpenter got up on his roan
And sallied from the gate in hell's despite
I heard him asking in the grimmest tone
If any enemy yet there was to fight?

"To any adversary it is fame
If he risk to be wounded by my tongue
Or burnt in two beneath my red heart's flame
Such are the perils he is cast among.

"But if he can he has a pretty choice
From an anatomy with little to lose
Whether he cut my tongue and take my voice
Or whether it be my round red heart he choose."

It was the neatest knave that ever was seen
Stepping in perfume from his lady's bower
Who at this word put in his merry mien
And fell on Captain Carpenter like a tower.

I would not knock old fellows in the dust
But there lay Captain Carpenter on his back
His weapons were the old heart in his bust
And a blade shook between rotten teeth alack.

The rogue in scarlet and grey soon knew his mind
He wished to get his trophy and depart
With gentle apology and touch refined
He pierced him and produced the Captain's heart.

God's mercy rest on Captain Carpenter now
I thought him Sirs an honest gentleman
Citizen husband soldier and scholar enow
Let jangling kites eat of him if they can.

But God's deep curses follow after those
That shore him of his goodly nose and ears
His legs and strong arms at the two elbows
And eyes that had not watered seventy years.

The curse of hell upon the sleek upstart
That got the Captain finally on his back
And took the red red vitals of his heart
And made the kites to whet their beaks clack clack.

—JOHN CROWE RANSOM

SIMPLE AUTUMNAL

The measured blood beats out the year's delay.
The tearless eyes and heart, forbidden grief,
Watch the burned, restless, but abiding leaf,
The brighter branches arming the bright day.

The cone, the curving fruit should fall away,
The vine stem crumble, ripe grain know its sheaf.
Bonded to time, fires should have done, be brief,
But, serfs to sleep, they glitter and they stay.

Because not last nor first, grief in its prime
Wakes in the day, and hears of life's intent.
Sorrow would break the seal stamped over time
And set the baskets where the bough is bent.

Full season's come, yet filled trees keep the sky
And never scent the ground where they must lie.

—LOUISE BOGAN

NOT WAVING BUT DROWNING

Nobody heard him, the dead man,
But still he lay moaning:
I was much further out than you thought
And not waving but drowning.

Poor chap, he always loved larking
And now he's dead
It must have been too cold for him his heart gave way,
They said.

Oh, no no no, it was too cold always
(Still the dead one lay moaning)
I was much too far out all my life
And not waving but drowning.

—STEVIE SMITH

LINES WRITTEN DURING A PERIOD OF INSANITY

Hatred and vengeance, my eternal portion,
Scarce can endure delay of execution:—
Wait, with impatient readiness, to seize my
     Soul in a moment.

Damn'd below Judas; more abhorr'd than he was,
Who, for a few pence, sold his holy master.
Twice betray'd, Jesus me, the last delinquent,
     Deems the profanest.

Man disavows, and Deity disowns me.
Hell might afford my miseries a shelter;
Therefore hell keeps her everhungry mouths all
     Bolted against me.

Hard lot! Encompass'd with a thousand dangers,
Weary, faint, trembling with a thousand terrors,
Fall'n, and if vanquish'd, to receive a sentence
     Worse than Abiram's:

Him, the vindictive rod of angry justice
Sent, quick and howling, to the centre headlong;
I, fed with judgments, in a fleshly tomb, am
     Buried above ground.

—WILLIAM COWPER

THE POET'S TASK

Whoever isn't listening to the sea this Friday
morning, whoever is trapped inside some
house, office, factory—or mistress
or street corner or coal mine or solitary confinement:
to that person I make my way and without speaking or nodding
come up and spring open the cage;
and something begins to hum, faint but insistent;
a great snapped-off clap of thunder harnesses itself
to the weight of the planet and the foam;
the hoarse rivers of the ocean rise up,
a star shimmers and trills in its rose window,
and the sea stumbles, falls, and continues on its way.

Then, with destiny as my pilot,
I will listen and listen harder to keep alive
in my memory the sea's outcry.
I must feel the impact of solid water
and save it in a cup outside of time
so that wherever anyone may be imprisoned,
wherever anyone is made to suffer in the dying year,
I will be there, whispering in the ceaseless tides.
I will drift through open windows,
and, hearing me, eyes will glance upward
saying, How can we get to the ocean?
And, without answering, I will pass on
the collapse of foam and liquid sand,
the salty kiss of withdrawal,
the gray keening of birds on the shore.
And so, through me, freedom and the sea
will bring solace to the downcast heart.

—PABLO NERUDA
translated by
Alfred Corn

A PLAGUE OF STARLINGS
(Fisk Campus)

Evenings I hear
the workmen fire
into the stiff
magnolia leaves,
routing the starlings
gathered noisy and
befouling there.

Their scissoring
terror like glass
coins spilling breaking
the birds explode
into mica sky
raggedly fall
to ground rigid
in clench of cold.

The spared return,
when the guns are through,
to the spoiled trees
like choiceless poor
to a dangerous
dwelling place,
chitter and quarrel
in the piercing dark
above the killed.

Mornings, I pick
my way past death's
black droppings:
on campus lawns
and streets

the troublesome
starlings
frost-salted lie,
troublesome still.

And if not careful
I shall tread
upon carcasses
carcasses when I
go mornings now
to lecture on
what Socrates,
the hemlock hour nigh,
told sorrowing
Phaedo and the rest
about the migratory
habits of the soul.

—ROBERT HAYDEN

Life, friends, is boring. We must not say so.
After all, the sky flashes, the great sea yearns,
we ourselves flash and yearn,
and moreover my mother told me as a boy
(repeatingly) "Ever to confess you're bored
means you have no

Inner Resources." I conclude now I have no
inner resources, because I am heavy bored.
Peoples bore me,
literature bores me, especially great literature,
Henry bores me, with his plights & gripes
as bad as achilles,

who loves people and valiant art, which bores me.
And the tranquil hills, & gin, look like a drag
and somehow a dog
has taken itself & its tail considerably away
into mountains or sea or sky, leaving
behind: me, wag.

—JOHN BERRYMAN

There sat down, once, a thing on Henry's heart
só heavy, if he had a hundred years
& more, & weeping, sleepless, in all them time
Henry could not make good.
Starts again always in Henry's ears
the little cough somewhere, an odour, a chime.

And there is another thing he has in mind
like a grave Sienese face a thousand years
would fail to blur the still profiled reproach of. Ghastly,
with open eyes, he attends, blind.
All the bells say: too late. This is not for tears;
thinking.

But never did Henry, as he thought he did,
end anyone and hacks her body up
and hide the pieces, where they may be found.
He knows: he went over everyone, & nobody's missing.
Often he reckons, in the dawn, them up.
Nobody is ever missing.

—JOHN BERRYMAN

THE INLAND LIGHTHOUSE

Into the night,
out from him,
out into the air
he throws his frames
and fixes them,
holds them out there.

These are his shores.
The waters never
rush at him, never
follow the beams
back along the watch
to his lean shiver.

Around him, as he
turns, he hears
a dull tick of grains.
He stares into the day.
Sand fills the sky
with its falling

and he turns and turns.
"Nowhere. Nowhere."
It is his oath.
He is the light,
the keeper.
He is not to leave.

—JAMES MCMICHAEL

KITCHENETTE BUILDING

We are things of dry hours and the involuntary plan,
Grayed in, and gray. "Dream" makes a giddy sound, not strong
Like "rent," "feeding a wife," "satisfying a man."

But could a dream send up through onion fumes
Its white and violet, fight with fried potatoes
And yesterday's garbage ripening in the hall,
Flutter, or sing an aria down these rooms

Even if we were willing to let it in,
Had time to warm it, keep it very clean,
Anticipate a message, let it begin?

We wonder. But not well! not for a minute!
Since Number Five is out of the bathroom now,
We think of lukewarm water, hope to get in it.

—GWENDOLYN BROOKS

SKUNK HOUR

(For Elizabeth Bishop)

Nautilus Island's hermit
heiress still lives through winter in her Spartan cottage;
her sheep still graze above the sea.
Her son's a bishop. Her farmer
is first selectman in our village;
she's in her dotage.

Thirsting for
the hierarchic privacy
of Queen Victoria's century,
she buys up all
the eyesores facing her shore,
and lets them fall.

The season's ill—
we've lost our summer millionaire,
who seemed to leap from an L. L. Bean
catalogue. His nine-knot yawl
was auctioned off to lobstermen.
A red fox stain covers Blue Hill.

And now our fairy
decorator brightens his shop for fall;
his fishnet's filled with orange cork,
orange, his cobbler's bench and awl;
there is no money in his work,
he'd rather marry.

One dark night,
my Tudor Ford climbed the hill's skull;
I watched for love-cars. Lights turned down,
they lay together, hull to hull,
where the graveyard shelves on the town. . . .
My mind's not right.

A car radio bleats,
"Love, O careless Love. . . ." I hear
my ill-spirit sob in each blood cell,
as if my hand were at its throat. . . .
I myself am hell;
nobody's here—

only skunks, that search
in the moonlight for a bite to eat.
They march on their soles up Main Street:
white stripes, moonstruck eyes' red fire
under the chalk-dry and spar spire
of the Trinitarian Church.

I stand on top
of our back steps and breathe the rich air—
a mother skunk with her column of kittens swills the garbage
    pail.
She jabs her wedge-head in a cup
of sour cream, drops her ostrich tail,
and will not scare.

—ROBERT LOWELL

MY MOTHER WOULD BE A FALCONRESS

My mother would be a falconress,
And I, her gay falcon treading her wrist,
would fly to bring back
from the blue of the sky to her, bleeding, a prize,
where I dream in my little hood with many bells
jangling when I'd turn my head.

My mother would be a falconress,
and she sends me as far as her will goes.
She lets me ride to the end of her curb
where I fall back in anguish.
I dread that she will cast me away,
for I fall, I mis-take, I fail in her mission.

She would bring down the little birds.
And I would bring down the little birds.
When will she let me bring down the little birds,
pierced from their flight with their necks broken,
their heads like flowers limp from the stem?

I tread my mother's wrist and would draw blood.
Behind the little hood my eyes are hooded.
I have gone back into my hooded silence,
talking to myself and dropping off to sleep.

For she has muffled my dreams in the hood she has made me,
sewn round with bells, jangling when I move.
She rides with her little falcon upon her wrist.
She uses a barb that brings me to cower.
She sends me abroad to try my wings
and I come back to her. I would bring down
the little birds to her
I may not tear into, I must bring back perfectly.

I tear at her wrist with my beak to draw blood,
and her eye holds me, anguisht, terrifying.
She draws a limit to my flight.
Never beyond my sight, she says.

She trains me to fetch and to limit myself in fetching.
She rewards me with meat for my dinner.
But I must never eat what she sends me to bring her.

Yet it would have been beautiful, if she would have carried me,
always, in a little hood with the bells ringing,
at her wrist, and her riding
to the great falcon hunt, and me
flying up to the curb of my heart from her heart
to bring down the skylark from the blue to her feet,
straining, and then released for the flight.

My mother would be a falconress,
and I her gerfalcon, raised at her will,
from her wrist sent flying, as if I were her own
pride, as if her pride
knew no limits, as if her mind
sought in me flight beyond the horizon.

Ah, but high, high in the air I flew.
And far, far beyond the curb of her will,
were the blue hills where the falcons nest.
And then I saw west to the dying sun—
it seemd my human soul went down in flames.

I tore at her wrist, at the hold she had for me,
until the blood ran hot and I heard her cry out,
far, far beyond the curb of her will

to horizons of stars beyond the ringing hills of the world where
    the falcons nest
I saw, and I tore at her wrist with my savage beak.
I flew, as if sight flew from the anguish in her eye beyond her
    sight,
sent from my striking loose, from the cruel strike at her wrist,
striking out from the blood to be free of her.

My mother would be a falconress,
and even now, years after this,
when the wounds I left her had surely heald,
and the woman is dead,
her fierce eyes closed, and if her heart
were broken, it is stilld

I would be a falcon and go free.
I tread her wrist and wear the hood,
talking to myself, and would draw blood.

—ROBERT DUNCAN

GET IT AGAIN

In 1978 I write something about how
happiness and sorrow are intertwined
and I feel good, insightful, and it seems
this reflects some healthy growth of spirit,
some deep maturation—then
I leaf through an eleven-year-old notebook
and spot some paragraphs I wrote in 1967
on Keats's "Ode on Melancholy" which
seem to say some of it better, or
almost better, or as well though differently—
and the waves roll out, and the waves roll in.

In 1972 I often ate rye toast with peanut butter,
the toast on a blue saucer beside my typewriter,
I took huge bites between paragraphs about love and change;
today it's a green saucer, cream cheese, French bread,
but the motions are the same and in a month or so
when the air is colder I'll be back to my autumn snack,
rye toast with peanut butter, an all-star since '72. . . .
I turned around on sidewalks to stare at women's asses
plenty of times in the sixties and
what do you think will be different in the eighties?
In 1970, mourning an ended love, I listened
to a sailor's song with a timeless refrain,
and felt better—that taste of transcendence
in the night air
and

and here it is in 1978, the night air, hello.

My journalist friend explains the challenge
of his new TV job: you work for a week
to get together one 5-minute feature,
and then
it's gone—
vanished into gray-and-white memory,
a fading choreography of electric dots—
and you're starting it all over,
every week that awesome energy demand:
to start over

In 1973 I played hundreds of games of catch
with a five-year-old boy named Brian.
Brian had trouble counting so we practiced
by counting the times we tossed the ball
without missing. When Brian missed
he was on the verge of despair for a moment
but I taught him to say
"Back to zero!" to give him a sense of
always another chance. I tried to make it sound
exciting to go back to zero, and eventually
our tone was exultant when we shouted in unison
after a bad toss or fumble
back to zero.

In 1977 I wrote a poem called "Repetition Rider"
and last winter I revised it three times
and I thought it was finished.

"It's not like writing," says my journalist friend,
"where your work is permanent—no matter how obscure,
written work is durable. . . . That's why
it can grow—you can move beyond
what you've already said."

Somewhere I read or heard something good
about what Shakespeare meant in *Lear*
when he wrote: "Ripeness is all."
I hope it comes back to me.
I see myself riding
the San Francisco subway in 1974
scrawling something in my little red notebook
about "getting nowhere fast"
I see Brian's big brown eyes lit
with the adventure of starting over
and oblivious, for a moment,
of the extent to which he is
doomed by his disabilities.
And the waves
roll out, and the waves roll in.
This poem

could go on a long time,
but you've already understood it;
you got the point some time ago,

and you'll get it again

—MARK HALLIDAY

BRILLIANCE

Maggie's taking care of a man
who's dying; he's attended to everything,
said goodbye to his parents,

paid off his credit card.
She says *Why don't you just
run it up to the limit?*

but he wants everything
squared away, no balance owed,
though he misses the pets

he's already found a home for
—he can't be around dogs or cats,
too much risk. He says,

I can't have anything.
She says, *A bowl of goldfish?*
He says he doesn't want to start

with anything and then describes
the kind he'd maybe like,
how their tails would fan

to a gold flaring. They talk
about hot jewel tones,
gold lacquer, say maybe

they'll go pick some out
though he can't go much of anywhere and then
abruptly he says *I can't love*

anything I can't finish.
He says it like he's had enough
of the whole scintillant world,

though what he means is
he'll never be satisfied and therefore
has established this discipline,

a kind of severe rehearsal.
That's where they leave it,
him looking out the window,

her knitting as she does because
she needs to do something.
Later he leaves a message:

Yes to the bowl of goldfish.
Meaning: let me go, if I have to,
in brilliance. In a story I read,

a Zen master who'd perfected
his detachment from the things of the world
remembered, at the moment of dying,

a deer he used to feed in the park,
and wondered who might care for it,
and at that instant was reborn

in the stunned flesh of a fawn.
So, Maggie's friend—
is he going out

into the last loved object
of his attention?
Fanning the veined translucence

of an opulent tail,
undulant in some uncapturable curve,
is he bronze chrysanthemums,

copper leaf, hurried darting,
doubloons, icon-colored fins
troubling the water?

—MARK DOTY

THAT EVENING AT DINNER

By the last few times we saw her it was clear
That things were different. When you tried to help her
Get out of the car or get from the car to the door
Or across the apartment house hall to the elevator
There was a new sense of heaviness
Or of inertia in the body. It wasn't
That she was less willing to be helped to walk
But that the walking itself had become less willing.
Maybe the stupid demogorgon blind
Recalcitrance of body, resentful of the laws
Of mind and spirit, was getting its own back now,
Or maybe a new and subtle, alien,
Intelligence of body was obedient now
To other laws: "Weight is the measure of
The force with which a body is drawn downward
To the center of the earth"; "Inertia is
The tendency of a body to resist
Proceeding to its fate in any way
Other than that determined for itself."

That evening, at the Bromells' apartment, after
She had been carried up through the rational structure
By articulate stages, floor after flashing floor,
And after we helped her get across the hall,
And get across the room to a chair, somehow
We got her seated in a chair that was placed
A little too far away from the nearest table,
At the edge of the abyss, and there she sat,
Exposed, her body the object of our attention—
The heaviness of it, the helpless graceless leg,
The thick stocking, the leg brace, the medical shoe.

At work between herself and us there was
A new principle of social awkwardness
And skillfulness required of each of us.
Our tones of voice in this easy conversation
Were instruments of marvelous finesse,
Measuring and maintaining with exactitude
"The fact or condition of the difference
There was between us, both in space and time."
Her smiling made her look as if she had
Just then tasted something delicious, the charm
Her courtesy attributed to her friends.

This decent elegant fellow human being
Was seated in virtue, character, disability,
Behind her the order of the ranged bookshelves,
The windows monitored by Venetian blinds—
"These can be raised or lowered; numerous slats,
Horizontally arranged, and parallel,
Which can be tilted so as to admit
Precisely the desired light or air."

We were all her friends, Maggie, and Bill, and Anne,
And I, and the nice Boston Brahmin elderly man
Named Duncan, utterly friendly and benign.
And of course it wasn't whether or not the world
Was benign but whether it looked at her too much.
She wasn't "painfully shy" but just the same
I wouldn't be surprised if there had been
Painfulness in her shyness earlier on,
Say at dancing school. Like others, though, she had
Survived her childhood somehow. Nor do I mean
She was unhappy. Maybe more or less so
Before her marriage. One had the sense of trips
Arranged, committees, concerts, baffled courage
Living it through, giving it order and style.

And one had the sense of the late marriage as of
Two bafflements inventing the sense they made
Together. The marriage seemed, to the outside world,
And probably was, radiant and triumphant,
And I think that one could almost certainly say
That during the last, heroic, phase of things,
After his death, and after the stroke, she had
By force of character and careful management,
Maintained a certain degree of happiness.

The books there on the bookshelves told their stories,
Line after line, all of them evenly spaced,
And spaces between the words. You could fall through the spaces.
In one of the books Dr. Johnson told the story:
"In the scale of being, wherever it begins,
Or ends, there are chasms infinitely deep;
Infinite vacuities . . . For surely,
Nothing can so disturb the passions, or
Perplex the intellects of man so much,
As the disruption of this union with
Visible nature, separation from all
That has delighted or engaged him, a change
Not only of the place but of the manner
Of his being, an entrance into a state
Not simply which he knows not, but perhaps
A state he has not faculties to know."

The dinner was delicious, fresh greens, and reds,
And yellows, produce of the season due,
And fish from the nearby sea; and there were also
Ashes to be eaten, and dirt to drink.

—DAVID FERRY

MEASURING THE TYGER

Barrels of chains. Sides of beef stacked in vans.
Water buffalo dragging logs of teak in the river mud
outside Mandalay. Pantocrater in the Byzantium dome.
The mammoth overhead crane bringing slabs of steel
through the dingy light and roar to the giant shear
that cuts the adamantine three-quarter-inch plates
and they flop down. The weight of the mind fractures
the girders and piers of the spirit, spilling out
the heart's melt. Incandescent ingots big as cars
trundling out of titanic mills, red slag scaling off
the brighter metal in the dark. The Monongahela River
below, night's sheen on its belly. Silence except
for the machinery clanging deeper in us. You will
love again, people say. Give it time. Me with time
running out. Day after day of the everyday.
What they call real life, made of eighth-inch gauge.
Newness strutting around as if it were significant.
Irony, neatness and rhyme pretending to be poetry.
I want to go back to that time after Michiko's death
when I cried every day among the trees. To the real.
To the magnitude of pain, of being that much alive.

—JACK GILBERT

THE DAY LADY DIED

It is 12:20 in New York a Friday
three days after Bastille day, yes
it is 1959 and I go get a shoeshine
because I will get off the 4:19 in Easthampton
at 7:15 and then go straight to dinner
and I don't know the people who will feed me

I walk up the muggy street beginning to sun
and have a hamburger and a malted and buy
an ugly NEW WORLD WRITING to see what the poets
in Ghana are doing these days
                              I go on to the bank
and Miss Stillwagon (first name Linda I once heard)
doesn't even look up my balance for once in her life
and in the GOLDEN GRIFFIN I get a little Verlaine
for Patsy with drawings by Bonnard although I do
think of Hesiod, trans. Richmond Lattimore or
Brendan Behan's new play or *Le Balcon* or *Les Nègres*
of Genet, but I don't, I stick with Verlaine
after practically going to sleep with quandariness

and for Mike I just stroll into the PARK LANE
Liquor Store and ask for a bottle of Strega and
then I go back where I came from to 6th Avenue
and the tobacconist in the Ziegfeld Theatre and
casually ask for a carton of Gauloises and a carton
of Picayunes, and a NEW YORK POST with her face on it

and I am sweating a lot by now and thinking of
leaning on the john door in the 5 SPOT
while she whispered a song along the keyboard
to Mal Waldron and everyone and I stopped breathing

—FRANK O'HARA

LADY LAZARUS

I have done it again.
One year in every ten
I manage it—

A sort of walking miracle, my skin
Bright as a Nazi lampshade,
My right foot

A paperweight,
My face a featureless, fine
Jew linen.

Peel off the napkin
O my enemy.
Do I terrify?—

The nose, the eye pits, the full set of teeth?
The sour breath
Will vanish in a day.

Soon, soon the flesh
The grave cave ate will be
At home on me

And I a smiling woman.
I am only thirty.
And like the cat I have nine times to die.

This is Number Three.
What a trash
To annihilate each decade.

What a million filaments.
The peanut-crunching crowd
Shoves in to see

Them unwrap me hand and foot—
The big strip tease.
Gentleman, ladies,

These are my hands
My knees.
I may be skin and bone,

Nevertheless, I am the same, identical woman.
The first time it happened I was ten.
It was an accident.

The second time I meant
To last it out and not come back at all.
I rocked shut

As a seashell.
They had to call and call
And pick the worms off me like sticky pearls.

Dying
Is an art, like everything else.
I do it exceptionally well.

I do it so it feels like hell.
I do it so it feels real.
I guess you could say I've a call.

It's easy enough to do it in a cell.
It's easy enough to do it and stay put.
It's the theatrical

Comeback in broad day
To the same place, the same face, the same brute
Amused shout:

"A miracle!"
That knocks me out.
There is a charge

For the eyeing of my scars, there is a charge
For the hearing of my heart—
It really goes.

And there is a charge, a very large charge
For a word or a touch
Or a bit of blood

Or a piece of my hair or my clothes.
So, so, Herr Doktor.
So, Herr Enemy.

I am your opus,
I am your valuable,
The pure gold baby

That melts to a shriek.
I turn and burn.
Do not think I underestimate your great concern.

Ash, ash—
You poke and stir.
Flesh, bone, there is nothing there—

A cake of soap,
A wedding ring,
A gold filling.

Herr God, Herr Lucifer,
Beware
Beware.

Out of the ash
I rise with my red hair
And I eat men like air.

—SYLVIA PLATH

SPITE—HOMAGE TO SYLVIA PLATH

I stamped my feet and shook my fist and wept,
I wanted to be one of that glamorous sorority of the dead,
to feel the rib cage opened, the knocking of the heart let out,
I wanted to lie with the paperweight of the Bible on my chest;
I wanted the return, the rebirth, to be the root you fell over,
the curb of earth that made you stumble. I wanted to be the little
poisonous selves that grew up in your gardens, the henbane,
and belladonna, the lovely, misnamed hens-and-chickens;
I wanted revenge, to be the meek inheriting, beyond hurt and worry,
I wanted to come back as the vegetal, the spectacular amphibian welter
of the swamp, the pond, the marsh, the fen, to begin again and again,
I wanted to be no mind, all flesh, no thinking, all feeling, just IS
taking everything into its bog, its tar pit, into the locked box of
    unbeing.

—LYNN EMANUEL

body

Look closely at the letters. Can you see,
entering (stage right), then floating full,
then heading off—so soon—
how like a little kohl-rimmed moon
o plots her course from *b* to *d*

—as *y*, unanswered, knocks at the stage door?
Looked at too long, words fail,
phase out. Ask, now that *body* shines
no longer, by what light you learn these lines
and what the *b* and *d* stood for.

—JAMES MERRILL

THE DEFINITION OF LOVE

My Love is of a birth as rare
As 'tis, for object, strange and high;
It was begotten by Despair
Upon Impossibility.

Magnanimous Despair alone
Could show me so divine a thing,
Where feeble Hope could ne'er have flown
But vainly flapped its tinsel wing.

And yet I quickly might arrive
Where my extended soul is fixed;
But Fate does iron wedges drive,
And always crowds itself betwixt.

For Fate with jealous eye does see
Two perfect loves, nor lets them close;
Their union would her ruin be,
And her tyrannic power depose.

And therefore her decrees of steel
Us as the distant poles have placed
(Though Love's whole world on us doth wheel),
Not by themselves to be embraced,

Unless the giddy heaven fall,
And earth some new convulsion tear,
And, us to join, the world should all
Be cramped into a planisphere.

As lines, so loves oblique may well
Themselves in every angle greet,
But ours, so truly parallel,
Though infinite, can never meet.

Therefore the love which us doth bind,
But Fate so enviously debars,
Is the conjunction of the mind,
And opposition of the stars.

—ANDREW MARVELL

TEACHERS

Pain is in this dark room like many speakers
of a costly set though mute
as here the needle and the turning

the night lengthens it is winter
a new year

what I live for I can seldom believe in
who I love I cannot go to
what I hope is always divided

but I say to myself you are not a child now
if the night is long remember your unimportance
sleep

then toward morning I dream of the first words
of books of voyages
sure tellings that did not start by justifying

yet at one time it seems
had taught me

—W. S. MERWIN

MEMORY UNSETTLED

Your pain still hangs in air,
Sharp motes of it suspended;
The voice of your despair—
That also is not ended:

When near your death a friend
Asked you what he could do,
"Remember me," you said.
We will remember you.

Once when you went to see
Another with a fever
In a like hospital bed,
With terrible hothouse cough
And terrible hothouse shiver
That soaked him and then dried him,
And you perceived that he
Had to be comforted,

You climbed in there beside him
And hugged him plain in view,
Though you were sick enough,
And had your own fears too.

—THOM GUNN

FRAGMENT

This time the hold up man didn't know a video-sound camera hidden
      up in a corner
was recording what was before it or more likely he didn't care, opening
      up with his pistol,
not saying a word, on the clerk you see blurredly falling and you hear
      —I keep hearing—
crying, "God! God!" in that voice I was always afraid existed within us,
      the voice that knows
beyond illusion the irrevocability of death, beyond any dream of being
      not mortally injured—
"You're just going to sleep, someone will save you, you'll wake again,
      loved ones beside you . . ."
Nothing of that: even torn by the flaws in the tape it was a voice that
      knew it was dying,
knew it was being—horrible—slaughtered, all that it knew and aspired
      to instantly voided;
such hopeless, astonished pleading, such overwhelmed, untempered pity
      for the self dying;
no indignation, no passion for justice, only woe, woe, woe, as he felt
      himself falling,
even falling knowing already he was dead, and how much I pray to
      myself I want not, ever,
to know this, how much I want to ask why I must, with such perfect,
      detailed precision,
know this, this anguish, this agony for a self departing wishing only to
      stay, to endure,
knowing all the while that, having known, I always will know this torn,
      singular voice
of a soul calling "God!" as it sinks back through the darkness it came
      from, cancelled, annulled.

—C. K. WILLIAMS

IN HOUSTON

I'd dislocated my life, so I went to the zoo.
It was December but it wasn't December. Pansies
just planted were blooming in well-groomed beds.
Lovers embraced under the sky's Sunday blue.
Children rode around and around on pastel trains.
I read the labels stuck on every cage the way
people at museums do, art being less interesting
than information. Each fenced-in plot had a map,
laminated with a stain to tell where in the world
the animals had been taken from. Rhinos waited
for rain in the rhino-colored dirt, too grief-struck
to move their wrinkles, their horns too weak
to ever be hacked off by poachers for aphrodisiacs.
Five white ducks agitated the chalky waters
of a duck pond with invisible orange feet
while a little girl in pink ruffles
tossed pork rinds at their disconsolate backs.

This wasn't my life! I'd meant to look
with the wise tough eye of exile, I wanted
not to anthropomorphize, not to equate, for instance,
the lemur's displacement with my displacement.
The arched aviary flashed with extravagance,
plumage so exuberant, so implausible, it seemed
cartoonish, and the birdsongs unintelligible,
babble, all their various languages unravelling—
no bird can get its song sung right, separated from
models of its own species.

For weeks I hadn't written a sentence,
for two days I hadn't spoken to an animate thing.
I couldn't relate to a giraffe—

I couldn't look one in the face.
I'd have said, if anyone had asked,
I'd been mugged by the Gulf climate.
In a great barren space, I watched a pair
of elephants swaying together, a rhythm
too familiar to be mistaken, too exclusive.
My eyes sweated to see the bull, his masterful trunk
swinging, enter their barn of concrete blocks,
to watch his obedient wife follow. I missed
the bitter tinny Boston smell of first snow,
the huddling in a cold bus tunnel.

At the House of Nocturnal Mammals,
I stepped into a furtive world of bats,
averted my eyes at the gloomy dioramas,
passed glassed-in booths of lurking rodents—
had I known I'd find what I came for at last?
How did we get here, dear sloth, my soul, my sister?
Clinging to a tree-limb with your three-toed feet,
your eyes closed tight, you calm my idleness,
my immigrant isolation. But a tiny tamarin monkey
who shares your ersatz rainforest runs at you,
teasing, until you move one slow, dripping,
hairy arm, then the other, the other, the other,
pulling your tear-soaked body, its too-few
vertebrae, its inferior allotment of muscles
along the dead branch, going almost nowhere
slowly as is humanly possible, nudged
by the bright orange primate taunting, nipping,
itching at you all the time, like ambition.

—GAIL MAZUR

"OUT, OUT—"

The buzz saw snarled and rattled in the yard
And made dust and dropped stove-length sticks of wood,
Sweet-scented stuff when the breeze drew across it.
And from there those that lifted eyes could count
Five mountain ranges one behind the other
Under the sunset far into Vermont.
And the saw snarled and rattled, snarled and rattled,
As it ran light, or had to bear a load.
And nothing happened: day was all but done.
Call it a day, I wish they might have said
To please the boy by giving him the half hour
That a boy counts so much when saved from work.
His sister stood beside them in her apron
To tell them "Supper." At the word, the saw,
As if to prove saws knew what supper meant,
Leaped out at the boy's hand, or seemed to leap—
He must have given the hand. However it was,
Neither refused the meeting. But the hand!
The boy's first outcry was a rueful laugh,
As he swung toward them holding up the hand,
Half in appeal, but half as if to keep
The life from spilling. Then the boy saw all—
Since he was old enough to know, big boy
Doing a man's work, though a child at heart—
He saw all spoiled. "Don't let him cut my hand off—
The doctor, when he comes. Don't let him, sister!"
So. But the hand was gone already.
The doctor put him in the dark of ether.
He lay and puffed his lips out with his breath.
And then—the watcher at his pulse took fright.

No one believed. They listened at his heart.
Little—less—nothing!—and that ended it.
No more to build on there. And they, since they
Were not the one dead, turned to their affairs.

—ROBERT FROST

THE YOKE

don't worry   I know you're dead
but tonight

turn your face again
toward me

when I hear your voice there is now
no direction in which to turn

I sleep and wake and sleep and wake and sleep and wake and

but tonight
turn your face again

toward me

see   upon my shoulders is the yoke
that is not a yoke

don't worry   I know you're dead
but tonight

turn your face again

—FRANK BIDART

THE WINDOW

Streak of world blurred charcoal & scarlet, the El slows,
brakes at the platform, Little Chinatown,
& there's that window, peeling frame, screen split

to rippling raingusts. A curtain breathes
through busted glass, a glimpse of hallway
enamelled green, rows of numbered doors, nothing more,

and then the train lurches forward sparkling
its electric signature above slick, hissing rails.
Soon, soon, I'll stop there, the window's pull

irresistible as the force of a star collapsed
to black gravity. I'll step through the window,
take up again the key for the one room to which

I keep returning. Let me wait again there by the sill
as I wait still. Here's the steeple of the burnt church,
beloved of vandals, the sooty block of

old law tenements where chipped tubs rise
porcelain on their feet in cold-water kitchens,
unashamed, small gray animals, the startled

array of insects we lived with.
Where are you? In the hallways, bodies passing
smell like bodies, unwashed, ginsoaked, dopesick,

the musk & salt. Where are you?
Hear with me the slant beat of that orthopedic shoe
striking pavement a few stained facades away.

With each echoing step, feel again the raw acceleration,
hope, or is it fear looming, receding?
Steaming hellmouths in the asphalt. If each of us

contains, within, humankind's totality, each possibility
then I have been so fractured, so multiple & dazzling
stepping towards myself through the room where

the New Year's dragon lies in its camphored sleep.
In the days I lived here, a thousand rooms
like it, making love was a way of saying *yes,*

I am here, these are my borders, hold me down
a little while. Make me real to myself. One more shining
thing gone after in the night that disappeared

with morning. No substance. But I'd like you
to place your hands, cradling the neck's swanny
arch, stand here by the copper dormer window

that's like an endless gallery of such windows
with fire escapes burdened by doves' insatiable
mourning. Then let it happen, the desire to be out

in the world, more than in it, wholly of it,
trammelled, broken to neoned figments.
All it takes is a few adjustments—

purple those lids, the lips as we did then,
that old mirror clouded with vague continents. We're
ready to inhabit the sequinned gowns, martini glasses

pouring their potions over the street, the milky syringes
& oh, those ravening embraces, the ravished streets
& whispered intersections. Slick back

the hair, and then the wig. I could never face anything
without the wig. Transformed, the old vaudeville desire
struts & kicks its satiny legs, the desire to be

consumed by ruined marquees, these last drifting hotels,
to be riven, served up singing, arched & prismed
from a thousand damp boulevards. Those things which shine

in the night, but what vertigo to surrender, falling
through the elaborate winged buildings they only have
in neighborhoods like this anymore, January's bitten snow

cold about the ankles. Let me move again, a wraith,
past these windows—bridesmaids' gowns the color
of casket linings, flammable, green

as gasoline poured from the can to flame the alley
outside the Welfare's fluorescent offices,
police stations, the shabby public hospital's endless

waiting rooms. How exactly pinned-to-the-wall
love was in that harsh economy, the world, the world, the world.
What I remember is the astringent sting of air.

Living on nothing but injections & vodka, a little
sugar. The self, multiple, dazzling. What I remember
are the coral husks of lobsters broken clean

through restaurant windows, steaming. Through these
windows tumble fragments, the stories, lavish
vertical fountains of opera. Dressed as death's-heads,

crowds demonstrate against the new war
with placards before the marble stairs. Like a wraith
let me move again among them, through the rooms

of this building, home of my fondest nightmares, let me
stay the hand twisting in rage, let me crush
the white & violet petals of sleep, the black sticky heart

of sleep over the delicate eyelids, over the bodies'
soft geographies, over the sorrow, the grandeur
of columns & esplanades, the soot-shouldered graces

outside the museum. Rude armfuls of orchids
fill the florist's windows, these lunar ones
curved like music staffs above dissolving aspirins

I might bring back to the room for you. Oh phantoms.
Oh the many lives that have fountained through
my own. Soon, soon, I shall stop upon that platform

& you will meet me there, the world rosegray beyond
the scalloped tops of buildings & we shall seek
that thing which shines & doth so much torment us.

—LYNDA HULL

ROUND

What was the need like driving rain
That struck the house and pelted the garden
So poorly planned? What was the creature
That needed to hide from the stunning torrent
Among the piers of the stone foundation
Under the house

That groaned in the wind? The seedlings floated
And spun in furrows that turned to runnels
Of muddy water while the hidden one watched
Apart from the ones that lived inside.
The house was pounded and stung by the wind
That flailed the siding

And pried at the roof. Though the beams looked sound
The rooms all shook. Who were the ones
Shaken inside and the one that hid
Among the stones all through the storm
While the whole failed garden melted to ruin?
What was the need?

—ROBERT PINSKY

MOCK ORANGE

It is not the moon, I tell you.
It is these flowers
lighting the yard.

I hate them.
I hate them as I hate sex,
the man's mouth
sealing my mouth, the man's
paralyzing body—

and the cry that always escapes,
the low, humiliating
premise of union—

In my mind tonight
I hear the question and pursuing answer
fused in one sound
that mounts and mounts and then
is split into the old selves,
the tired antagonisms. Do you see?
We were made fools of.
And the scent of mock orange
drifts through the window.

How can I rest?
How can I be content
when there is still
that odor in the world?

—LOUISE GLÜCK

PERSONALS

Some nights I sleep with my dress on. My teeth
are small and even. I don't get headaches.
Since 1971 or before, I have hunted a bench
where I could eat my pimento cheese in peace.
If this were Tennessee and across that river, Arkansas,
I'd meet you in West Memphis tonight. We could
have a big time. Danger, shoulder soft.
Do not lie or lean on me. I am still trying to find a job
for which a simple machine isn't better suited.
I've seen people die of money. Look at Admiral Benbow. I wish
like certain fishes, we came equipped with light organs.
Which reminds me of a little known fact:
if we were going the speed of light, this dome
would be shrinking while we were gaining weight.
Isn't the road crooked and steep.
In this humidity, I make repairs by night. I'm not one
among millions who saw Monroe's face
in the moon. I go blank looking at that face.
If I could afford it I'd live in hotels. I won awards
in spelling and the Australian crawl. Long long ago.
Grandmother married a man named Ivan. The men called him
Eve. Stranger, to tell the truth, in dog years I am up there.

—C. D. WRIGHT

HOW I GOT THIS WAY

Our knees were knobby on linoleum,
Donnie's and mine, and it was our worst
moment ever though we never knew for sure
what curse had caused it. I think
it was our mother reading *The family*
that prays together stays together
somewhere, but there we were

on a regular Tuesday night
when I was eight, a night
like any other—the kind
of night that starts out good, my brother
Donnie and I flicking peas across the dinner
table while Mama and Daddy fought
about his buddy Rudy, who hung around
our place too much and who was divorcing
his reasonable wife. That

was the kind of night it was, a good night
like any other, when my mother put her fork down
and announced that we were going to say
the rosary together *as a family*
on Tuesday nights with the radio
tuned to a program called "Family Rosary Hour."
We were horrified, but when

Mom walked toward that radio,
her body slanted with purpose,
we knew there was no way out of it. When she
said that we all should kneel then, on our own
living room floor, near the record player
and the Monopoly game, in front of each other

on a Tuesday, I saw my brother's errant
eyebrow begin the dance which meant
that he was cornered and life was turning smelly.

The floor squeaked beneath our knees
as radio voices leapt into our house;
embraced by roiling static they prayed like
a chorus of bees. Mama was the first among us
to join them. I watched her lips moving
and listened, aghast at how my own mother's
voice had merged with the voices in the static—
those bees— as if she weren't actually
one of us after all, but was some kind of spy.
I considered reporting her.

And even though the rest of us resisted,
we were eventually lassoed by her eye, till
in the end all the voices in our house
had joined the voices of the bees that prayed
across the airwaves. I could see neighbors

out the window in the blue evening street
throwing balls and washing cars, being normal.
We knelt there for years that night, avoiding
one another's eyes, praying and staying
together, murder in our hearts; caught
in holy static like travelers in a fog,
led by the pale beacon of my mother's voice
together toward some promised land
she'd always dreamed of.

                                —PATRICIA TRAXLER

FRIENDS WHO HAVE FAILED

They leave from positions of strength, like all baroque
civilizations; leave the statues we cannot imagine moving
for heaviness caught in the skirts . . .
We watch their gestures grow finer and more nervous
in the widening air.
They are the best judges of wine; talk always at the glittering
    edges
of things, the terrible auras . . . The afternoons in their houses
hang upside down, like objects seen through wine.
Their footfalls die an inch away in the carpet.

And leaving, we wonder why the world
has not appreciated this fineness; why clumsier juggling
finds favor in its slow eye . . .
But we have not understood the world; how its way
is to destroy without destroying, the way air
levels a mountain; things fly apart in a vacuum . . .
It wears us to the hard thing we cannot help being;
and if the only hard thing is our determination
not to be hard, it wears us down to that.

—ALAN WILLIAMSON

"BOY 'CARRYING-IN' BOTTLES IN GLASS WORKS"

West Virginia, 1911
Photograph by Lewis W. Hine

What makes his face heartbreaking
is that he wouldn't have it so—
just one of many boys working
amid splinters of glass that throw
such light they seem its only source
in this dusky photograph.
A random instant of the past.
And the brutal factory, of course,

is only one memory of brutality
on the world's infinite list.
The boy would now be over eighty,
retired, unnoticed,
but surely he was stunted and is dead.
It's this look of his—
like a word almost said—
across an unchartable distance,

that shapes and bends
emotion toward him now,
though he wouldn't have it so.
He just looked into a lens
amid splinters of glass that throw
such light they seem its only source,
and rods and chutes that criss-cross
like some malign, unnameable force.

—MICHAEL RYAN

WATCHING *SHOAH* IN A HOTEL ROOM IN AMERICA

There are nights as soft as fur on a foal
but we prefer chess or card playing. Here,
some hotel guests sing "Happy Birthday"
as the one-eyed TV nonchalantly shuffles its images.
The trees of my childhood have crossed an ocean
to greet me coolly from the screen.
Polish peasants engage with a Jesuitical zest
in theological disputes: only the Jews are silent,
exhausted by their long dying.
The rivers of the voyages of my youth flow
cautiously over the distant, unfamiliar continent.
Hay wagons haul not hay, but hair,
their axles squeaking under the feathery weight.
We are innocent, the pines claim.
The SS officers are haggard and old,
doctors struggle to save them their hearts, lives, consciences.
It's late, the insinuations of drowsiness have me.
I'd sleep but my neighbors
choir "Happy Birthday" still louder:
louder than the dying Jews.
Huge trucks transport stars from the firmament,
gloomy trains go by in the rain.
I am innocent, Mozart repents;
only the aspen, as usual, trembles,
prepared to confess all its crimes.
The Czech Jews sing the national anthem: "Where is my home . . ."
There is no home, houses burn, the cold gas whistles within.
I grow more and more innocent, sleepy.
The TV reassures me: both of us
are beyond suspicion.
The birthday is noisier.
The shoes of Auschwitz, in pyramids

high as the sky, groan faintly:
Alas, we outlived mankind, now
let us sleep, sleep:
we have nowhere to go.

—ADAM ZAGAJEWSKI
translated by
Renata Gorczynski, Benjamin Ivry,
and C. K. Williams

DOLOR

I have known the inexorable sadness of pencils,
Neat in their boxes, dolor of pad and paper-weight,
All the misery of manilla folders and mucilage,
Desolation in immaculate public places,
Lonely reception room, lavatory, switchboard,
The unalterable pathos of basin and pitcher,
Ritual of multigraph, paper-clip, comma,
Endless duplication of lives and objects.
And I have seen dust from the walls of institutions,
Finer than flour, alive, more dangerous than silica,
Sift, almost invisible, through long afternoons of tedium,
Dropping a fine film on nails and delicate eyebrows,
Glazing the pale hair, the duplicate gray standard faces.

—THEODORE ROETHKE

INSOMNIA

The almost disturbing scent
of peonies presses through the screens,
and I know without looking how
those heavy white heads lean down
under the moon's light. A cricket chafes
and pauses, chafes and pauses,
as if distracted or preoccupied.

When I open my eyes to document
my sleeplessness by the clock, a point
of greenish light pulses near the ceiling.
A firefly . . . In childhood I ran out
at dusk, a jar in one hand, lid
pierced with airholes in the other,
getting soaked to the knees
in the long wet grass.

The light moves unsteadily, like someone
whose balance is uncertain after traveling
many hours, coming a long way.
Get up. Get up and let it out.

But I leave it hovering overhead, in case
it's my father, come back from the dead
to ask, "Why are you still awake? You can
put grass in their jar in the morning."

—JANE KENYON

FACING IT

My black face fades,
hiding inside the black granite.
I said I wouldn't,
dammit: No tears.
I'm stone. I'm flesh.
My clouded reflection eyes me
like a bird of prey, the profile of night
slanted against morning. I turn
this way—the stone lets me go.
I turn that way—I'm inside
the Vietnam Veterans Memorial
again, depending on the light
to make a difference.
I go down the 58,022 names,
half-expecting to find
my own in letters like smoke.
I touch the name Andrew Johnson;
I see the booby trap's white flash.
Names shimmer on a woman's blouse
but when she walks away
the names stay on the wall.
Brushstrokes flash, a red bird's
wings cutting across my stare.
The sky. A plane in the sky.
A white vet's image floats
closer to me, then his pale eyes
look through mine. I'm a window.
He's lost his right arm
inside the stone. In the black mirror
a woman's trying to erase names:
No, she's brushing a boy's hair.

—YUSEF KOMUNYAKAA

OLD JOKE

Radiant child of Leto, far working Lord Apollo,
with lyre in hand and golden plectrum, you sang to the gods
on Mount Olympus almost as soon as you were born.

You sang, and the Muses sang in answer, and together
your voices so delighted all your deathless elders
that their perfect happiness was made more perfect still.

What was it, though, that overwhelmed them, that suffused,
astonished, even the endless aether? Was it the freshest,
most wonderful stops of breath, the flawless intervals

and scales whose harmonies were mimicking in sound
the beauty of the gods themselves, or what you joined
to that, what you were singing of, our balked desires,

the miseries we suffer at your indifferent hands,
devastation, and bereavement, old age and death?
Farworking, radiant child, what do you know about us?

Here is my father, half blind, and palsied, at the toilet,
he's shouting at his penis, Piss, you! Piss! Piss!
but the penis (like the heavenly host to mortal prayers)

is deaf and dumb; here, too, my mother with her bad knee,
on the eve of surgery, hobbling by the bathroom,
pausing, saying, who are you talking to in there?

and he replies, no one you would know, sweetheart.
Supernal one, in your untested mastery,
your easy excellence, with nothing to overcome,

and needing nothing but the most calamitous
and abject stories to prove how powerful you are,
how truly free, watch them as they laugh so briefly,

godlike, better than gods, if only for a moment
in which what goes wrong is converted to a rightness,
if only because now she's hobbling back to bed

where she won't sleep, if only because he pees at last,
missing the bowl, and has to get down on his knees
to wipe it up. You don't know anything about us.

—ALAN SHAPIRO

LAMENTATION ON UR

2,000 B.C.

Like molten bronze and iron shed blood
      pools. Our country's dead
melt into the earth
      as grease melts in the sun, men whose
helmets now lie scattered, men annihilated

by the double-bladed axe. Heavy, beyond
      help, they lie still as a gazelle
exhausted in a trap,
      muzzle in the dust. In home
after home, empty doorways frame the absence

of mothers and fathers who vanished
      in the flames remorselessly
spreading claiming even
      frightened children who lay quiet
in their mother's arms, now borne into

oblivion, like swimmers swept out to sea
      by the surging current.
May the great barred gate
      of blackest night again swing shut
on silent hinges. Destroyed in its turn,

may this disaster too be torn out of mind.

               —TOM SLEIGH

OZYMANDIAS

I met a traveler from an antique land
Who said: Two vast and trunkless legs of stone
Stand in the desert . . . Near them, on the sand,
Half sunk, a shattered visage lies, whose frown,
And wrinkled lip, and sneer of cold command,
Tell that its sculptor well those passions read
Which yet survive, stamped on these lifeless things,
The hand that mocked them, and the heart that fed:
And on the pedestal these words appear:
"My name is Ozymandias, king of kings:
Look on my works, ye Mighty, and despair!"
Nothing beside remains. Round the decay
Of that colossal wreck, boundless and bare
The lone and level sands stretch far away.

—PERCY BYSSHE SHELLEY

THEY FEED THEY LION

Out of burlap sacks, out of bearing butter,
Out of black bean and wet slate bread,
Out of the acids of rage, the candor of tar,
Out of creosote, gasoline, drive shafts, wooden dollies,
They Lion grow.
        Out of the gray hills
Of industrial barns, out of rain, out of bus ride,
West Virginia to Kiss My Ass, out of buried aunties,
Mothers hardening like pounded stumps, out of stumps,
Out of the bones' need to sharpen and the muscles' to stretch,
They Lion grow.
        Earth is eating trees, fence posts,
Gutted cars, earth is calling in her little ones,
"Come home, Come home!" From pig balls,
From the ferocity of pig driven to holiness,
From the furred ear and the full jowl come
The repose of the hung belly, from the purpose
They Lion grow.
        From the sweet glues of the trotters
Come the sweet kinks of the fist, from the full flower
Of the hams the thorax of caves,
From "Bow Down" come "Rise Up,"
Come they Lion from the reeds of shovels,
The grained arm that pulls the hands,
They Lion grow.
        From my five arms and all my hands,
From all my white sins forgiven, they feed,
From my car passing under the stars,
They Lion, from my children inherit,

From the oak turned to a wall, they Lion,
From they sack and they belly opened
And all that was hidden burning on the oil-stained earth
They feed they Lion and he comes.

—PHILIP LEVINE

MEMPHIS BLUES

Nineveh, Tyre,
Babylon,
Not much lef'
Of either one.
All dese cities
Ashes and rust,
De win' sing sperrichals
Through deir dus' . . .
Was another Memphis
Mongst de olden days,
Done been destroyed
In many ways. . . .
Dis here Memphis
It may go;
Floods may drown it;
Tornado blow;
Mississippi wash it
Down to sea—
Like de other Memphis in
History.

2

Watch gonna do when Memphis on fire,
    Memphis on fire, Mistah Preachin' Man?
Gonna pray to Jesus and nebber tire,
    Gonna pray to Jesus, loud as I can,
        Gonna pray to my Jesus, oh, my Lawd!

Watcha gonna do when de tall flames roar,
   Tall flames roar, Mistah Lovin' Man?
Gonna love my brownskin better'n before—
    Gonna love my baby lak a do right man,
      Gonna love my brown baby, oh, my Lawd!

Watcha gonna do when Memphis falls down,
   Memphis falls down, Mistah Music Man?
Gonna plunk on dat box as long as it soun',
    Gonna plunk dat box fo' to beat de ban',
      Gonna tickle dem ivories, oh, my Lawd!

Watcha gonna do in de hurricane,
   In de hurricane, Mistah Workin' Man?
Gonna put dem buildings up again,
    Gonna put em up dis time to stan',
      Gonna push a wicked wheelbarrow, oh, my Lawd!

Watcha gonna do when Memphis near gone,
   Memphis near gone, Mistah Drinkin' Man?
Gonna grab a pint bottle of Mountain Corn,
    Gonna keep de stopper in my han',
      Gonna get a mean jag on, oh, my Lawd!

Watcha gonna do when de flood roll fas',
   Flood roll fas', Mistah Gamblin' Man?
Gonna pick up my dice fo' one las' pass—
    Gonna fade my way to de lucky lan',
      Gonna throw my las' seven—oh, my Lawd!

3

Memphis go
By Flood or Flame;
Nigger won't worry
All de same—
Memphis go
Memphis come back,
Ain' no skin
Off de nigger's back.
All dese cities
Ashes, rust. . . .
De win' sing sperrichals
Through deir dus'.

—STERLING A. BROWN

NIGHT WASH

All seas are seas in the moon to these
lonely and full of light.
High above laundries and rooftops
the pinstriped silhouettes speak nightmare
as do the faces full of fire and orange peel.
Every citizen knows what's the trouble: *America's longest*
river is—New York; that's what they say, and I say so.

Wonderful thing, electricity,
all these neons and nylons spun dry by a dime
in the Fifth Street Laundromat. The city
must be flying a thousand kites tonight
with its thousands of different keys.
—Sir, excuse me, *sir?*
Excuse me interfering, but you don't want
to put that in—it's got a rubber backing, see? Oh, not at all . . .

Piles of workshirts, piles of leopard underthings,
it's like fishing upside down all night long, and then the moon
    rises
like armfuls of thready sleeves. Her voice
rising and falling, her boys folded sideways asleep on the bench:
—Listen, that old West Indian cleaning lady?
Ask anyone here, she never has change.
Come on, she's too wise . . .

Down in the Tombs
the prisoner's knuckles climb like stripes
of paint in the light. He dreams he hears
the voice of a pig he used to slop for his uncles.
It pokes its head
through the bars and says
"Have you brought any beet greens?"

—You can never leave them alone at night. Like today
the stitching overseer says to me
If you can't keep the rhythm missus . . .
I says to him fire
me all you want, I don't take that shit
off anybody. That was a scare though—
you can't always get back on a day shift.

In the moonlight
the city rides serenely enough, its thousand light moorings
the hunted news in their eyes. Even the rivers
are tidal, as sailors and bankers know.
The glass bank of the Chase Manhattan stands dark
over the Harbor. One last
light slowly moving around the top floor.

—No washing machines in the basement, that's
what's the trouble. The laundry would dry overnight
on the roof, in the wind. Well a month ago
you know, some big boys took this twelveyearold
little Spanish girl up there. Then they killed her, they
threw her, six stories down. Listen, the stone age or something
running around on those roofs. So this cop said to me
Your street is the bottom, he actually
said that to me. So what could I say—that it's great?

On the folding table the same
gestures repeat, smoothing and folding
the same ancient shirt. Or the old West Indian cleaning lady
pretending to finger her pockets for change. At midnight she'll prop
her grey spaghetti mop and glide toward you
in her black cotton trousers, her black
lavender face tilted up. Very clearly
she says to the world in dream-language
I mean to live.

—ANNE WINTERS

MY GRANDMOTHER'S LOVE LETTERS

There are no stars to-night
But those of memory.
Yet how much room for memory there is
In the loose girdle of soft rain.

There is even room enough
For the letters of my mother's mother,
Elizabeth,
That have been pressed so long
Into a corner of the roof
That they are brown and soft,
And liable to melt as snow.

Over the greatness of such space
Steps must be gentle.
It is all hung by an invisible white hair.
It trembles as birch limbs webbing the air.

And I ask myself:

"Are your fingers long enough to play
Old keys that are but echoes:

Is the silence strong enough
To carry back the music to its source
And back to you again
As though to her?"

Yet I would lead my grandmother by the hand
Through much of what she would not understand;
And so I stumble. And the rain continues on the roof
With such a sound of gently pitying laughter.

—HART CRANE

THE WEARY BLUES

Droning a drowsy syncopated tune,
Rocking back and forth to a mellow croon,
    I heard a Negro play.
Down on Lenox Avenue the other night
By the pale dull pallor of an old gas light
    He did a lazy sway . . .
    He did a lazy sway . . .
To the tune o' those Weary Blues.
With his ebony hands on each ivory key
He made that poor piano moan with melody.
    O Blues!
Swaying to and fro on his rickety stool
He played that sad raggy tune like a musical fool.
    Sweet Blues!
Coming from a black man's soul.
    O Blues!
In a deep song voice with a melancholy tone
I heard that Negro sing, that old piano moan—
    "Ain't got nobody in all this world,
    Ain't got nobody but ma salf.
    I's gwine to quit ma frownin'
    And put ma troubles on the shelf."
Thump, thump, thump, went his foot on the floor.
He played a few chords then he sang some more—
    "I got the Weary Blues
    And I can't be satisfied.
    Got the Weary Blues
    And can't be satisfied—
    I ain't happy no mo'
    And I wish that I had died."
And far into the night he crooned that tune.

The stars went out and so did the moon.
The singer stopped playing and went to bed
While the Weary Blues echoed through his head.
He slept like a rock or a man that's dead.

—LANGSTON HUGHES

ELEGY ON THE DEATH OF SIDNEY

Silence augmenteth grief, writing increaseth rage,
Staled are my thoughts, which loved, & lost, the wonder of our age;
Yet quickened now with fire, though dead with frost ere now,
Enraged I write, I know not what: dead, quick, I know not how.

Hard hearted minds relent and rigor's tears abound,
And envy strangely rues his end, in whom no fault she found,
Knowledge her light hath lost, valor hath slain her knight,
Sidney is dead, dead is my friend, dead is the world delight.

Place pensive wails his fall, whose presence was her pride,
Time crieth out, my ebb is come: his life was my spring tide,
Fame mourns in that she lost the ground of her reports,
Each living wight laments his lack, and all in sundry sorts.

He was (woe worth that word) to each well thinking mind,
A spotless friend, a matchless man, whose vertue ever shined,
Declaring in his thoughts, his life, and that he writ,
Highest conceits, longest foresights, and deepest works of wit.

He only like himself, was second unto none,
Whose death (though life) we rue, & wrong, & all in vain do moan,
Their loss, not him wail they, that fill the world with cries,
Death slew not him, but he made death his ladder to the skies.

Now sink of sorrow I, who live, the more the wrong,
Who wishing death, whom death denies, whose thread is all too long,

Who tied to wretched life, who looks for no relief,
Must spend my ever dying days, in never ending grief.

Heart's ease and only I, like parallels run on,
Whose equal length keep equal breadth, & never meet in one;
Yet for not wronging him, my thoughts, my sorrow's cell,
Shall not run out, though leak they will, for liking him so well.

Farewell to you my hopes, my wonted waking dreams,
Farewell somtimes enjoyed ioy, eclipsed are thy beams,
Farewell self pleasing thoughts, which quietness brings forth,
And farewell friendship's sacred league, uniting minds of worth;

And farewell merry heart, the gift of guiltless minds,
And all sports, which for life's restore, variety assigns,
Let all that sweet is, void: in me no mirth may dwell,
Philip, the cause of all this woe, my life's content farewell.

Now rime, the son of rage, which art no kin to skill,
And endles grief, which deads my life, yet knows not how to kill,
Go seek that hapless tomb, which if ye hap to find,
Salute the stones, that keep the limbs, that held so good a mind.

—EDWARD DYER

RALEGH'S HISTORY OF THE WORLD, AN EPITAPH FOR BENT

Plato's Longing was more decorous than mine—
difference marked the distance from fulfillment,
the measure of love was the depth of its incapacity

—no clowns like me ignoring the law
holding the gaze of a dying animal, likely
scaring her with my grief, saying
I love you, the chant over and over becoming a song
of helplessness across floating waters,
the tiny boat floating away on pure weakness,
caught in a placid tide; and I,
Picture of Sincerity, Body of Devotion
carried on.

Some would compare this grief to others
and find it slight among the world of cares
but I rebel against that measure
and seek a way to bring this heart to bear

—there was in you a consciousness of me,
your eyes sought mine so carefully,
and as you sank within the deepest of the seas
that I loved you and that you could love me
was simple.

Experience and Truth, twinned virtues, flank the bellied
breasted woman holding up the world, her head
surrounded by the shooting fires of the sun;
Good Fame and Bad Fame blow horns above a globe
whose botched continents show what we know by now—
Experience is sad, and Veritas is beautiful.

—SUZANNE QUALLS

SONG ON PORCELAIN

Rose-colored cup and saucer,
Flowery demitasses:
You lie beside the river
Where an armored column passes.
Winds from across the meadow
Sprinkle the banks with down;
A torn apple tree's shadow
Falls on the muddy path;
The ground everywhere is strewn
With bits of brittle froth—
Of all things broken and lost
Porcelain troubles me most.

Before the first red tones
Begin to warm the sky
The earth wakes up, and moans.
It is the small sad cry
Of cups and saucers cracking,
The masters' precious dream
Of roses, of mowers raking,
And shepherds on the lawn.
The black underground stream
Swallows the frozen swan.
This morning, as I walked past,
The porcelain troubled me most.

The blackened plain spreads out
To where the horizon blurs
In a litter of handle and spout,
A lively pulp that stirs
And crunches under my feet.
Pretty, useless foam:

Your stained colors are sweet,
Spattered in dirty waves
Flecking the fresh black loam

In the mounds of these new graves.
In sorrow and pain and cost,
Sir, porcelain troubles me most.

Washington, D.C., 1947
—CZESŁAW MIŁOSZ
translated by Robert Pinsky

MID-TERM BREAK

I sat all morning in the college sick bay
Counting bells knelling classes to a close.
At two o'clock our neighbours drove me home.

In the porch I met my father crying—
He had always taken funerals in his stride—
And Big Jim Evans saying it was a hard blow.

The baby cooed and laughed and rocked the pram
When I came in, and I was embarrassed
By old men standing up to shake my hand

And tell me they were "sorry for my trouble."
Whispers informed strangers I was the eldest,
Away at school, as my mother held my hand

In hers and coughed out angry tearless sighs.
At ten o'clock the ambulance arrived
With the corpse, stanched and bandaged by the nurses.

Next morning I went up into the room. Snowdrops
And candles soothed the bedside; I saw him
For the first time in six weeks. Paler now,

Wearing a poppy bruise on his left temple,
He lay in the four foot box as in his cot.
No gaudy scars, the bumper knocked him clear.

A four foot box, a foot for every year.

—SEAMUS HEANEY

ON MY FIRST SON

Farewell, thou child of my right hand, and joy;
My sin was too much hope of thee, lov'd boy:
Seven years thou wert lent to me, and I thee pay,
Exacted by thy fate, on the just day.
Oh, could I lose all father, now! for why,
Will man lament the state he should envy?
To have so soon 'scaped world's, and flesh's rage,
And, if no other misery, yet age!
Rest in soft peace, and ask'd, say here doth lie
BEN JONSON his best piece of poetry:
For whose sake henceforth all his vows be such,
As what he loves may never like too much.

—BEN JONSON

WAVING GOOD-BY

I wanted to know what it was like before we
had voices and before we had bare fingers and before we
had minds to move us through our actions
and tears to help us over our feelings,
so I drove my daughter through the snow to meet her friend
and filled her car with suitcases and hugged her
as an animal would, pressing my forehead against her,
walking in circles, moaning, touching her cheek,
and turned my head after them as an animal would,
watching helplessly as they drove over the ruts,
her smiling face and her small hand just visible
over the giant pillows and coat hangers
as they made their turn into the empty highway.

—GERALD STERN

ELEGY FOR JANE
My Student, Thrown by a Horse

I remember the neckcurls, limp and damp as tendrils;
And her quick look, a sidelong pickerel smile;
And how, once startled into talk, the light syllables leaped for
    her,
And she balanced in the delight of her thought,
A wren, happy, tail into the wind,
Her song trembling the twigs and small branches.
The shade sang with her;
The leaves, their whispers turned to kissing;
And the mold sang in the bleached valleys under the rose.

Oh, when she was sad, she cast herself down into such a pure
    depth,
Even a father could not find her:
Scraping her cheek against straw;
Stirring the clearest water.

My sparrow, you are not here,
Waiting like a fern, making a spiny shadow.
The sides of wet stones cannot console me,
Nor the moss, wound with the last light.

If only I could nudge you from this sleep,
My maimed darling, my skittery pigeon.
Over this damp grave I speak the words of my love:
I, with no rights in this matter,
Neither father nor lover.

—THEODORE ROETHKE

LAST HIRED

On Monday returned the man I fired
wanting the phone number of the laborer he loaned money to,
and stood while I wrote it out on a scrap of shingle
and the crew on the floor kept hammering

with the silence of three hammers tapping out different beats.
I scratched down the name and seven digits with a flat pencil
scrawling across the ridged grain and then with it.
He thanked me with an uncomfortable smile and left.

He was incompetent, but incompetence is not a crime
—I never liked him.
Out of almost pure intuition, right from the beginning
and I noticed how quickly the other men closed in beside me

against him. He must have felt it, too,
those days as he knocked the nails out of his screwed-up formwork,
and spit saliva in the hammermarks of his windowsills
to raise the grain. Must have every day

felt more alone. He had a habit of mumbling explanations
that trailed into incoherence. But he was not a stupid man.
When I asked him to repeat himself, he shrugged me off
with a sigh and asked me what I wanted him to do.

The morning I fired him I walked down to the street
before he could leave his truck, and was on the way surprised
and annoyed by a hypocritical watering in my eyes that went away.
Then catching him, saw-in-hand, I told him to go back to the truck.

I said it deliberately hard, so he would guess
before I said the words. Then we stood together. And he took it
as if he expected, and failure were something he had grown around.
Then he got in his truck, drove the street, and was gone.

—MARK TURPIN

After great pain, a formal feeling comes—
The Nerves sit ceremonious, like Tombs—
The stiff Heart questions was it He, that bore,
And Yesterday, or Centuries before?

The Feet, mechanical, go round—
Of Ground, or Air, or Ought—
A Wooden way
Regardless grown,
A Quartz contentment, like a stone—

This is the Hour of Lead—
Remembered, if outlived,
As Freezing persons, recollect the Snow—
First—Chill—then Stupor—then the letting go—

—EMILY DICKINSON

ENGLISH I

FIRST, We tied to each other
NEXT, Coconuts for the swimming
THEN, The Boat-Soldiers shoot
MEANWHILE, Many dying
AND THEN, We swam with dead People
LATER, We get on the land
FINALLY, We left our dead Friends.

What grade does this exercise deserve?
Homework folded like a handkerchief,
a little book of tears, burns, escape—

And still I mark the blasphemies
of punctuation, common speech;
the English tune will help them live.

Rickety Hmong boy, flirting simply
with the loud girl from Managua—
I taught him how to ask her out,

taught her how to say no, nicely;
my accent and suburban decorums
are tidy and authoritative as

the checks I make for right answers,
the rosy golf-clubs on the page.
By next year they'll talk their way

out of trouble instead of smiling
as they do hearing me drone *Silent Night*—
They join in, shy and hypnotized,

Saigon chemist, cowed Haitian, miming
the words I once told my music teacher
that Jews shouldn't sing: "Holy Infant."

—DAVID GEWANTER

BODY, REMEMBER. . . .

Body, remember not only how much you were loved,
not only the beds you lay on,
but also those desires that glowed openly
in eyes that looked at you,
trembled for you in the voices—
only some chance obstacle frustrated them.
Now that it's all finally in the past,
it seems almost as if you gave yourself
to those desires too—how they glowed,
remember, in eyes that looked at you,
remember, body, how they trembled for you in those voices.

> —CONSTANTINE CAVAFY
> translated by Edmund Keeley
> and Phillip Sherrard

CORTÈGE

Do not imagine you can abdicate
                                Auden

Prologue

If the sea could dream, and if the sea
were dreaming now, the dream
would be the usual one: Of the Flesh.
The letter written in the dream would go
something like: *Forgive me — love, Blue.*

I. The Viewing (A Chorus)

O what, then, did he look like?
>   He had a good body.

And how came you to know this?
>   His body was naked.

Say the sound of his body.
>   His body was quiet.

Say again—quiet?
>   He was sleeping.

You are sure of this? Sleeping?
>   Inside it, yes, Inside it.

II. Pavilion

Sometimes, a breeze: a canvas
flap will rise and, inside,
someone stirs; *a bird? a flower?*

One is thinking *Should there be*
thirst, I have only to reach
for the swollen bag of skin

beside me, I have only to touch
my mouth that is meant for a flower
to it, and drink.

One is for now certain he is
one of those poems that stop only;
they do not end.

One says without actually saying it
I am sometimes a book of such poems,
I am other times a flower and lovely

pressed like so among them, but
always they forget me.
I miss my name.

They are all of them heat-
weary, anxious for evening as for
some beautiful to the bone

messenger to come. They will open
again for him. His hands are good.
His message is a flower.

III. *The Tasting (A Chorus)*

O what, then, did he taste like?
> He tasted of sorrow.

And how came you to know this?
> My tongue still remembers.

Say the taste that is sorrow.
> Game, fallen unfairly.

And yet, you still tasted?
> Still, I tasted.

Did you say to him something?
> I could not speak, for hunger.

IV. Interior

And now,
the candle blooms gorgeously away
from his hand—

and the light has made
blameless all over
the body of him (mystery,

mystery), twelvefold
shining, by grace of twelve
mirrors the moth can't stop

attending. Singly, in no order,
it flutters against, beats
the glass of each one,

as someone elsewhere
is maybe beating upon
a strange door now,

somebody knocks
and knocks at a new
country, of which

nothing is understood—
no danger occurs
to him, though

danger could be any
of the unusually wild
flowers

that, either side of the road,
spring.
When he slows, bends down and

closer, to see or
to take one—it is as if
he knows something to tell it.

V. *The Dreaming (A Chorus)*

O what, then, did it feel like?
                              I dreamed of an arrow.

And how came you to know him?
                              I dreamed he was wanting.

Say the dream of him wanting.
                              A swan, a wing folding.

Why do you weep now?
                    I remember.

Tell what else you remember.
                         The swan was mutilated.

Envoi

And I came to where was nothing but drowning
and more drowning, and saw to where the sea—
besides flesh—was, as well, littered with boats;
how each was blue but trimmed with white, to each
a name I didn't know and then, recalling,
did. And ignoring the flesh that, burning, gives
more stink than heat, I dragged what boats I could
to the shore and piled them severally in a tree-
less space, and lit a fire that didn't take
at first—the wood was wet—and then, helped by
the wind, became a blaze so high the sea
itself, along with the bodies in it, seemed
to burn. I watched as each boat fell to flame:
Vincent and *Matthew* and, last, what bore your name.

—CARL PHILLIPS

A LITANY IN TIME OF PLAGUE

Adieu, farewell, earth's bliss;
This world uncertain is;
Fond are life's lustful joys;
Death proves them all but toys;
None from his darts can fly;
I am sick, I must die.
   Lord, have mercy on us!

Rich men, trust not in wealth,
Gold cannot buy you health;
Physic himself must fade.
All things to end are made,
The plague full swift goes by;
I am sick, I must die
   Lord, have mercy on us!

Beauty is but a flower
Which wrinkles will devour;
Brightness falls from the air;
Queens have died young and fair;
Dust hath closed Helen's eye.
I am sick, I must die.
   Lord, have mercy on us!

Strength stoops unto the grave.
Worms feed on Hector brave;
Swords may not fight with fate,
Earth still holds ope her gate.
"Come, come!" the bells do cry.
I am sick, I must die.
   Lord, have mercy on us.

Wit with his wantonness
Tasteth death's bitterness;
Hell's executioner
Hath no ears for to hear
What vain art can reply.
I am sick, I must die.
    Lord, have mercy on us.

Haste, therefore, each degree,
To welcome destiny;
Heaven is our heritage,
Earth but a player's stage;
Mount we unto the sky.
I am sick, I must die.
    Lord, have mercy on us.

—THOMAS NASHE

THE BUSINESS OF FANCYDANCING

After driving all night, trying to reach
Arlee in time for the fancydance
finals, a case of empty
beer bottles shaking our foundations, we
stop at a liquor store, count out money,
and would believe in the promise

of any man with a twenty, a promise
thin and wrinkled in his hand, reach-
ing into the window of our car. Money
is an Indian Boy who can fancydance
from powwow to powwow. We
got our boy, Vernon WildShoe, to fill our empty

wallets and stomachs, to fill our empty
cooler. Vernon is like some promise
to pay the light bill, a credit card we
Indians get to use. When he reach-
es his hands up, feathers held high, in a dance
that makes old women speak English, the money

for first place belongs to us, all in cash, money
we tuck in our shoes, leaving our wallets empty
in case we pass out. At the modern dance,
where Indians dance white, a twenty is a promise
that can last all night long, a promise reach-
ing into back pockets of unfamiliar Levis. We

get Vernon there in time for the finals and we
watch him like he was dancing on money,
which he is, watch the young girls reach-
ing for him like he was Elvis in braids and an empty
tipi, like Vernon could make a promise
with every step he took, like a fancydance

could change their lives. We watch him dance
and he never talks. It's all a business we
understand. Every drum beat is a promise
note written in the dust, measured exactly. Money
is a tool, putty to fill all the empty
spaces, a ladder so we can reach

for more. A promise is just like money.
Something we can hold, in twenties, a dream we reach.
It's business, a fancydance to fill where it's empty.

—SHERMAN ALEXIE

TICHBORNE'S ELEGY

Written with his own hand
in the tower before his execution

My prime of youth is but a frost of cares,
My feast of joy is but a dish of pain,
My crop of corn is but a field of tares,
And all my good is but vain hope of gain;
The day is past, and yet I saw no sun,
And now I live, and now my life is done.

My tale was heard and yet it was not told,
My fruit is fallen and yet my leaves are green,
My youth is spent and yet I am not old,
I saw the world and yet I was not seen;
My thread is cut and yet it is not spun,
And now I live, and now my life is done.

I sought my death and found it in my womb,
I looked for life and saw it was a shade,
I trod the earth and knew it was my tomb,
And now I die, and now I was but made;
My glass is full, and now my glass is run,
And now I live, and now my life is done.

—CHIDIOCK TICHBORNE

CHURCH MONUMENTS

While that my soul repairs to her devotion,
Here I intomb my flesh, that it betimes
May take acquaintance of this heap of dust;
To which the blast of death's incessant motion,
Fed with the exhalation of our crimes,
Drives all at last. Therefore I gladly trust

My body to this school, that it may learn
To spell his elements, and find his birth
Written in dusty heraldry and lines;
Which dissolution sure doth best discern,
Comparing dust with dust, and earth with earth.
These laugh at jet, and marble put for signs,

To sever the good fellowship of dust,
And spoil the meeting. What shall point out them,
When they shall bow, and kneel, and fall down flat
To kiss those heaps, which now they have in trust?
Dear flesh, while I do pray, learn here thy stem
And true descent, that when thou shalt grow fat

And wanton in they cravings, thou mayst know
That flesh is but the glass which holds the dust
That measures all our time; which also shall
Be crumbled into dust. Mark, here below
How tame these ashes are, how free from lust,
That thou mayst fit thyself against thy fall.

—GEORGE HERBERT

MADAME LA FLEURIE

Weight him down, O side-stars, with the great weightings of
      the end.
Seal him there. He looked in a glass of the earth and thought he
      lived in it.
Now, he brings all that he saw into the earth, to the waiting
      parent.
His crisp knowledge is devoured by her, beneath a dew.

Weight him, weight, weight him with the sleepiness of the
      moon.
It was only a glass because he looked in it. It was nothing he
      could be told.
It was a language he spoke, because he must, yet did not know.
It was a page he had found in the handbook of heartbreak.

The black fugatos are strumming the blacknesses of black . . .
The thick strings stutter the finial gutturals.
He does not lie there remembering the blue-jay, say the jay.
His grief is that his mother should feed on him, himself and
      what he saw,
In that distant chamber, a bearded queen, wicked in her dead
      light.

—WALLACE STEVENS

WHAT HE THOUGHT

for Fabbio Doplicher

We were supposed to do a job in Italy
and, full of our feeling for
ourselves (our sense of being
Poets from America) we went
from Rome to Fano, met
the mayor, mulled
a couple matters over (what's
cheap date, they asked us; what's
flat drink). Among Italian literati

we could recognize our counterparts:
the academic, the apologist,
the arrogant, the amorous,
the brazen and the glib—and there was one

administrator (the conservative), in suit
of regulation gray, who like a good tour guide
with measured pace and uninflected tone narrated
sights and histories the hired van hauled us past.
Of all, he was most politic and least poetic,
so it seemed. Our last few days in Rome
(when all but three of the New World Bards had flown)
I found a book of poems this
unprepossessing one had written: it was there
in the *pensione* room (a room he'd recommended)
where it must have been abandoned by
the German visitor (was there a bus of *them?*)
to whom he had inscribed and dated it a month before.
I couldn't read Italian, either, so I put the book
back into the wardrobe's dark. We last Americans

were due to leave tomorrow. For our parting evening then
our host chose something in a family restaurant, and there
we sat and chatted, sat and chewed,
till, sensible it was our last
big chance to be poetic, make
our mark, one of us asked
                        "What's poetry?
Is it the fruits and vegetables and
marketplace of Campo dei Fiori, or
the statue there?" Because I was

the glib one, I identified the answer
instantly, I didn't have to think—"The truth
is both, it's both," I blurted out. But that
was easy. That was easiest to say. What followed
taught me something about difficulty,
for our underestimated host spoke out,
all of a sudden, with a rising passion, and he said:

The statue represents Giordano Bruno,
brought to be burned in the public square
because of his offense against
authority, which is to say
the Church. His crime was his belief
the universe does not revolve around
the human being: God is no
fixed point or central government, but rather is
poured in waves through all things. All things
move. "If God is not the soul itself, He is
the soul of the soul of the world." Such was
his heresy. The day they brought him
forth to die, they feared he might
incite the crowd (the man was famous
for his eloquence). And so his captors
placed upon his face
an iron mask, in which

he could not speak. That's
how they burned him. That is how
he died: without a word, in front
of everyone.
              And poetry—
                              (we'd all
put down our forks by now, to listen to
the man in gray; he went on
softly)—
              poetry is what
he thought, but did not say.

                    —HEATHER MCHUGH

PERMISSIONS

808. 81 Han

The handbook of heartbre
ak :
$18. 00 02/19/99 AGE-9301